GROWING INTO MY WINGS

By Mel Hoehne

DISCLAIMER

This book is a work of non-fiction, but certain aspects have been altered or disguised to protect the privacy and identities of real-life individuals. While every effort has been made to accurately represent the events and experiences documented within these pages, the names, descriptions, and specific details of individuals and events have been changed or modified to safeguard the anonymity of those involved.

The author and publisher have taken meticulous care to ensure that the identities and circumstances described in this book bear no direct connection to any real persons, living or deceased. Any perceived similarities to actual individuals or situations are entirely coincidental and unintentional.

This work is a true account of the author's experiences and observations, but the alterations made to names, descriptions, and events are intended solely to protect the privacy and confidentiality of individuals. The author does not seek to harm, defame, or infringe upon the rights of any person or entity.

Growing Into My Wings
© Mel Hoehne 2023

ISBN: 978-1-922784-90-2 (Paperback)

Self-published by Mel Hoehne
Proudly printed in Australia by Clark & Mackay

This book is dedicated to my inner child,

To the girl I once was,

To the girl who dreamed about becoming the woman I am today,

To the girl who needed to learn that true beauty comes from within,

To the girl who holds emotions, memories and beliefs from the past, To the girl who hopes and dreams for the future,

To the little caterpillar waiting on her metamorphosis.

And to all those beautiful women out there who still struggle to find their worth. You are enough!

PRELUDE | BETRAYAL

It wasn't until I learned of my husband's betrayal that I could see clearly. Up until that moment I truly believed that we lived a dream life. I believed that he was the love of my life, and I was his. Of course, no relationship is without its ups and downs, but this almost broke me. Almost.

I am a very trusting and loyal person, maybe even naïvely trusting. I would never expect someone to do something bad. Trust is something you build, something that comes with hard work, love, reliability and truth. Trust is putting your insecurities to rest and leaning into the safety of the bond you have formed with another person. Trust makes us vulnerable, which is why it's not something that just happens.

When that trust is broken by the people who love you, and should be protecting you at any cost, all your buried, hidden insecurities come rushing back. Every unsure feeling you've ever had about yourself resurfaces and doubt creeps in…

CHAPTER ONE | UNSEEN

"In the midst of winter, I found there was, within me, an invincible summer."

— Albert Camus, *Invincible Summer*

Growing up in my small, picturesque home town in Germany as the middle child of a relatively normal family, I always felt like an outsider. It was the type of town where you are known, but not seen, and that was how I felt within my family as well. I simply didn't fit into what they wanted me to be. Both my siblings seemed to excel at what my parents thought they should be good at, while I needed to be pushed into all those things. Of course, in the society where I grew up, girls weren't really seen as people that could 'do it for themselves'.

My mum was always at home, cleaning, gardening and cooking. She was there when we got home from school and consistently ensured we were well fed, looked neat and tidy and did the chores or school work required of us.

Before I was born, my mum had worked as a florist and she never lost her love for green things and gardening. She was an ideal stay at home mum – constantly cleaning, cooking, baking and making our home look good. She was always outside digging in the dirt, planting seeds, new flowers and various plants. She created an enchanted garden, with not a single weed in sight. Everything was spotless, always. She had a lovely creativity in her but I wonder now if she ever missed working or if she was disappointed that she was compelled to stay at home because of the children. She never complained, but she never shared any happy thoughts about it either. Communication wasn't something that I was used to growing up.

My dad was benevolently quiet, silently ensuring that we got the best he could provide for us. While he was at work or tinkering in the garage for much of my childhood, he always turned up when we needed him.

He taught me how to ride a bike, how to swim and later how to drive a car. He often took us to the forest to chop wood for the cold winter months and my brother and I had picnics and built treehouses while he worked. I can clearly remember the smell of freshly cut wood and I can still hear the sound of the chainsaw. I loved those times. My mum usually stayed home, cooked up a storm and brought food to us in the forest.

My dad never took a long break, he ate his meal quickly and went on with his job. He is to date the most hardworking man I know. I never ever heard him complain and he was always working on something or for someone and never asked for anything in return. Always humble and kind.

First day of school with my Schultüte - Age 6

I have such wonderful childhood memories of my dad, but there is one that remains very special to me today. When I was about six or seven-years-old, I really wanted the Peaches and Cream Barbie. For a long time, it's all I had wished for. Everyday when my dad came home, I would ask him: "Did you bring me something? Do you have anything for me?" He'd say to me: "Melli, I don't go to the toy store when I have to work."

At the time, my dad was working for a construction company, driving big machines. So obviously he wasn't going to the toy store on his way from work. One day before my birthday, he came home, put his work bag in the hallway as usual and said to me: "Go have a look in my bag, there is something for you." I remember it as if it was yesterday – I ran to his bag and looked inside to find the Barbie in its box. I will remember this moment forever and ever. This meant the world to me.

It's one of my favourite childhood memories, not just because I got the doll that I dreamed and talked about every day, but because I thought that my dad had gone to the toy store for me. Even though we lived a very simple life, money was never an issue. I always got what I wanted or needed. So it meant more to me that he actually stopped by the toy store then getting the Barbie I wanted.

I would find out years later that my mum was actually the one who bought the Barbie and put it in his bag. But at the time, he got the full credit. My mum never said a thing about it, probably because she knew this was a huge moment for me.

My parents wanted me to have a musical education – that was their way of allowing for my creativity, when all I wanted was to dress up and experiment with my clothes.

I learned to play numerous instruments, yet hated every minute of it. It's interesting that when you are not aligned with something in your soul, you are blind to the advantages it might give you. Like learning music – so many people in the world would have loved that opportunity, but because it simply wasn't something I desired, I hated it. I had a private lesson once a week with a music teacher and had to practise for an hour everyday after school. I would always try to get out of it with no success. So instead, I would record myself playing the clarinet on a cassette tape, lock my door and play back the recordings while I wrote love stories in my diary or browsed the fashion catalogues.

My mum forced me to stick with it and always said I'd thank her one day. I didn't understand it at the time, but now I know that it taught me about persistence and success. I learned that if you do the hard things that you don't like, leave your comfort zone sometimes and never give up, you can be extremely successful. I never wanted to be a successful musician, but if I gave up learning music back then I don't think I would be as persistent as I am today. I would not have had the strength to pull through many tough situations in my life.

I have always been fascinated with fashion. From as young as four, I always needed to have an outfit change – at least two during a typical day. I remember my whole family laughing when I changed my outfit; they never took me seriously, even if they could see that this really made me feel good. It's that fascination with fashion that created the spark and ignited my passion. It's a passion that continues to drive me today. I still get changed at least twice a day. That's my way of expressing creativity and style.

Although I knew I was loved by my parents, in their different ways, I was never really given the words of encouragement that I think I needed. Many years later, I learned that we are all different in how we give and receive love. We all have different love languages and if we don't understand them, it can have a major impact on how we relate to other people. Looking back, I can see today that they were always showing me love in the best way they could.

Emotions, feelings and words are what move me, I always felt that. Always. Yet I felt like I couldn't always share my feelings while growing up. I couldn't share what I wanted to do. That contributed to my feelings of never being enough. I continually tried to be perfect in a world where everyone expected certain things of me while I never expected anything in return.

At my eighth birthday party, I had a few girlfriends around for the afternoon and my sister set up games for us to play in the backyard. All my friends were better than I was at the games – I lost at every game. I felt like everyone had fun and that they made fun of me for losing. Nobody commented or encouraged me and being my birthday, I guess I expected a little bit of favouritism. So, I ended up in tears because I was upset at losing so spectacularly on my special day.

Seeing this, my mum sent all my friends home and told them to take their presents with them. I was devastated and felt completely humiliated. I then had to go to each of their homes to apologise for my bad behaviour. It's something that still triggers me when I think about it today: *Always be on your best behaviour, never show your true feelings, don't complain, swallow your emotions, and don't be a burden to anyone.* Ever since then, I don't like celebrating my birthday, and still get emotional every year. I also keep my expectations low every birthday to avoid any disappointment.

My dad was more approachable, even though he worked long hours and we rarely saw him until late at night. Whenever I got bad grades on my report card, I'd wait for him to come home so he could sign it. He always did so without any comments except to tell me to do better next time.

My mum, on the other hand, would immediately question me about what my peers had scored and then berate me for not doing as well as them. On the flip side, if I did happen to get better marks than the average and pointed this out to her, she'd tell me not to compare myself to others. My achievements weren't celebrated, only my failings were highlighted and scrutinised. Today I understand that all they ever wanted was the best for me; to have a great life and do well. They were just pushing me to do better and work harder.

Adding to my feelings of being an outsider, at around age 15, all my friends had already started their periods. But, being small and skinny for my age, I guess I was a late starter. My mum questioned me a number of times, asking if I'd 'got it' yet. She never used the word "period" and didn't explain to me what it was about at all – she probably assumed I knew from my friends. She bought me all the necessary supplies and put them in the bathroom and kept asking me if I had started yet. When I didn't, she said that there must be something wrong with me. I woke up most mornings for a long time praying that my period would begin so I could be just like everyone else.

The result was that I didn't feel like I was achieving. I felt 'less than' all the way through my childhood. It wasn't just the music; I just didn't fit into what society and my family thought I should be like. So many people experience that, and when it comes to women, that almost becomes the norm, where they are not allowed to be who they really are. I was told I should get a qualification in something to do with admin or secretarial work. Maybe my parents were hoping I would meet a stable man at the office that would sweep me off my feet and take me off their hands.

Naturally, and unfavourably, I was always compared to my sister, the eldest, who is incredibly smart. She was the first grandchild who was a girl and she was the angel. She could do no wrong. She was amazing at everything she did. She had the best grades in school, she could play almost every instrument and could sing as well. And she enjoyed it all. She was insanely creative and interested in literally everything. Because she was nine years older than me, I looked up to her and admired her for everything she did, had and created. I never wanted to be like her, but I adored her for loving what she was doing. And she was incredibly good at it. I could never quite understand why I wasn't able to do the things I loved and be praised for it, like my sister.

When my little brother came along, he, like many youngest children, had slightly different rules and expectations. He was super cute, and a boy, so I once again didn't quite make the grade. He was a wild child though, always in trouble, he was rough and loud, but had a huge heart. I remember one snowy evening in December, St. Nikolaus turned up at our balcony door (my sister's boyfriend at the time had dressed up) and got us some presents for St. Nikolaus day. I gave him a neat picture that I'd drawn. And my brother, with his big heart, gave him a 2DM coin (we still had Deutschmark back then) to contribute to the gifts he brought us. For years, this was the top story in our family every Christmas.

I was different – I loved dressing up my Barbie dolls. I got lost in the world of fashion and style. I would always be experimenting with clothes, like removing sleeves from dresses to create matching accessories like belts, handbags or headbands. I mixed up different colours and materials and always watched my mum on the sewing machine.

I was inspired by Barbie and I dreamed of a life as a successful businesswoman with her own car and house, and amazing clothes. But most importantly, living life the way she wants to and making her own decisions. Being a mum with two children was also something I always pictured for my life.

I imagined working in a hotel, seeing new people every day and interacting with travellers who were excited to explore the world. My entire childhood I dreamt of travelling to exotic places; I could see myself wandering around beautiful spaces wearing all the latest fashion. Meeting incredible people, being recognised for something I'd created. I thought about working for a travel agency where I could recommend different destinations and learn about all the extraordinary parts of this planet. It seemed like a dream too far when I was growing up.

I loved reading and writing, it was one of the few subjects I was actually good at. Since written words were such a massive part of my life growing up, I always wanted to write love stories about princesses and horses. I loved writing down my feelings and then locking them up and hiding my diary in my room; I was a little afraid someone could find it and read my thoughts. I always knew that one day I would write a book.

As a teenager, I did the usual teen things – I had a number of girlfriends that I hung out with, and to say that I was a huge fan of a particular popular boy band at the time, is an understatement. So many of the guys I had crushes on were those that looked a bit like the lead singer – longish, blonde hair and really cute. I even got to meet the band when I was 18.

I had my first kiss when I was 15 and I remember it so clearly. It was one of the most embarrassing and uncomfortable moments ever. He was two years older than me and dreamily cute. I was the only girl in school that hadn't been kissed yet. We were at his house and I knew it was going to happen. I wanted it to happen, I needed it to happen. At the time, it felt like a task, something I just had to finally do, so I could be part of the conversations with the girls at school.

I was really nervous and my whole body broke out in hives – red patches everywhere. I could feel the heat waves and ran into the bathroom, trying to calm my nerves and soothe my skin with cold water. For me the kiss was kind of gross and I didn't enjoy it. I can't even remember the guy's name, he did look like my boy band crush, but I wasn't really interested in him being my boyfriend. I don't think we met again after that day. My first kiss was just something to tick off the list of things I wanted to experience.

Although I spent all of my childhood immersed in fashion and experimenting with style, when it came to choosing a career, I felt stuck. Growing up in the 80s, my mum convinced me that I needed to work in an office. Work in an office, get married, have children and become a stay-at-home-mum – that was the expectation, right? It's what my mum did, and she found her dream job, the thing she was good at was being a mum and she didn't even get paid for it.

My mum convinced me that I needed to earn my own money and the best way to do that was with an office job. I didn't understand it as a teenager because I wanted to do something with fashion. But that wasn't seen as a "real job" by society's standards. I now understand that my mum wanted me to have an office job so that I would have it easier, but it wasn't communicated that way.

I started an apprenticeship in an office where I'd make coffee, sort folders and make copies all day long. I hated it. The only thing I did like about it was the opportunity to wear nice office clothes everyday. It was like having my own little fashion show each day when I went to work. The work itself gave me no satisfaction or enjoyment. It just made no sense to me. Plus, my grades were so bad that I decided to break off my apprenticeship half way through my exams.

My mum talked me out of working in a hotel, saying that I would have to clean toilets and that clearly wasn't the job for me. I was 17 at the time and went to a career counsellor for guidance. In their waiting room there were information flyers about working as an au pair overseas, all expenses paid for 12 months. It included flights and a small weekly allowance. It sounded ideal for me since I had always dreamed of exploring the world. I signed up to become an au pair for an American family. Much to my mother's distaste.

Before I left for the States I'd been taking a dancing course with a few of my friends and my brother and I decided to set up a disco in his room one night. He had an incredible sound system and we got a smoke machine to create a disco atmosphere.

My brother and I had a few friends over to enjoy the disco. Some of them brought a few extra friends too – that's how I met Stephanie. She was the "loud one" – very extroverted and unconventional. I told her about my plans to go to America and she was amazed. Even though she was such an outgoing, extroverted person, she was also very family-orientated. She admired my guts to pack my bags and go out into the big world outside of our small, German hometown. I didn't see it at the time, but Stephanie was to become a very important part of my life in later years.

The 12 months I spent exploring the United States had a massive impact on me since I was away from home for the first time and I was only 18 – I was basically still a kid. My English was not the best and I didn't know anything about looking after children. However, I was living with an amazing family and got to learn about different cultures and traditions.

I looked after three children under the age of three and it was a tough responsibility but I loved it! That year came with a lot of struggles and challenges, living with a foreign family, experiencing homesickness for the first time – especially when I spoke to my mum on the phone. We didn't have social media like we do today so the only way to stay in touch was by phone or email. On the positive side, I discovered my love for children, I made so many new connections and learned how to cope on my own and express my feelings and emotions.

For the first time I was able to let go of what was, and learned how to grow from a little shy girl into an independent woman. It really changed me and broadened my horizons.

Since I was such a big fan of the boy band, I made it my mission to go to every possible concert that I could during my time in America. They were super popular in Germany at the time but hadn't achieved the same level of fame in America yet. They were so unknown that the CD shop had to specially order their CD for me because they had no idea who the band was.

I was thrilled that I also got the chance to meet my celebrity crush, the lead singer of the boy band, while I was there. Since the band was based in Florida, I flew down there with two other au pairs during our two week holiday. We rented a car and did a road trip around Florida. We chased them up at a few places. I knew all their hiding spots and secret places. I was so determined to meet the lead singer, that I flew down to Florida again for three days by myself to find him. I spent all the money I earned from au pairing to book flights and a hotel. Before I left, my host mum asked me how I was going to find him and I simply responded by saying "I'll figure it out."

When I got to Tampa, I found a phone booth and went through the phone book ringing up every single family with his last name, with no luck. I had a photo of him that I took through every fast food restaurant and supermarket, asking if anyone knew him – no one recognised him! I was shocked that no one knew who he was; he was such a famous guy with the band in Germany, he lives here in Tampa, these people should know who he is. On the verge of giving up, with hardly any money left and running out of time, I went back to my hotel room and called my host mum to update her, crying: "I'll never find him." She asked me if I had opened the envelope she gave me before I left; I hadn't opened it, so she told me to look inside. She had put $200 and a note in it for me. The note wished me good luck and to look after myself. And there was an address... my celebrity crush's address!

My host mum was a police detective, so she knew all the right ways to find his address and she sent it with me. I called a taxi to take me there since I was still too young to rent a car in the States. I told the taxi driver everything on the way to the singer's house and when we got there he said he'd wait for me and I assured him I was fine and he could go. Of course, I was thinking that he would invite me in and it would all be fine. But since I didn't have a mobile phone and no way to contact anyone, he convinced me that he would wait.

I went up and rang the doorbell of this big mansion in the middle of nowhere. Someone answered and I just asked for him to come outside and see me. And they asked who I was and I said "I'm from Germany, I'm a fan." The voice on the other side said, "Okay, hold on a sec." Five minutes later, there he was. He was walking towards me. I couldn't believe it! There I was, this little kid from Germany meeting my celebrity crush. Everyone back home told me I was crazy for trying to find him. People asked: "what do you think Mel, you just rock up at his house and he comes out and says hi?" Yes, that's what I thought and here I was, standing right in front of him. He asked me where I was from and when I told him I came from Germany, he was shocked: "What? Where did you get my address from?" I replied "Oh, I just figured it out."

I gave him a letter and some chocolates, and the taxi driver took a photo of us – thankfully he had waited for me. Back then we still had film cameras so I had to wait three weeks to see if the photo was good or not. After we said goodbye, I was in an absolute trance, I really just went to his house and met him. The taxi driver took my arm and guided me back to the taxi and took me back to my hotel.

A few months later, I met him again! A friend of mine from Germany was visiting and stayed with me and my host family for two weeks. We went to a concert of theirs in the city at this small town hall. Compared to the concerts in Germany it was tiny – only about 300 people and the tickets only cost about $20 (we used to pay about DM200 in Germany). We were walking around the hall trying to find a way to get backstage when this bus pulled up and all the band members got out with their crew and bodyguards. We had made a sign that said "Germany loves you" and when they saw it they knew that we were true fans.

It was still hours before the concert so there weren't too many people there yet, when we were approached by someone from the local radio station. He asked us if we were attending the concert and if we would like to go backstage and have a meet-and-greet with the band. Of course we said yes! We couldn't believe our luck. Once backstage, they signed our CD and asked if we would like to go up on stage during the show and dance with the boys. I asked to be paired up with the lead singer, my friend and another girl got paired up with two of the other band members, and the remaining band members would sing.

We were sitting in the third row just two metres from the stage so we could easily get to it when a specific song came on. It was a dream come true! As part of the show, we had to sit and have a conversion with our dance partner. Once I was sitting across from him, he said to me: "I know you, I've seen you before." I told him yes, I'm from Germany. And he asked: "Did you come to my house?"

He remembered me! The moment passed so quickly and before I knew it the song was over, he handed me a red rose and we were heading back into the audience. I kept that rose for years, and I had it tattooed on my left shoulder before I left the States. That night my friend said to me: "Mel, no one will ever believe that story." And she was right.

I ended up meeting them on a few more occasions at local events. It was the best experience ever. It made me realise that if you believe in your dreams, if you have something that you really want, like I wanted to meet my celebrity crush, if you're persistent enough you can reach those dreams. Well, I didn't end up marrying him, but meeting him, going backstage and dancing with him on stage were incredible moments that I will hold in my heart forever. My little boy band mission was a very important part of my year in America.

During those 12 months, I didn't feel like I had to consistently perform a role that wasn't meant for me. I looked after the kids and had fun with them – that was all I was expected to do. There was nobody judging me or making me feel 'less than'. For the first time in as long as I could remember, I was okay with who I was.

When I returned to Germany, I was a very different person because I had seen something of the world and experienced different people and attitudes. I realised then that there was a big world out there and that I simply didn't have to remain within the confines of my small town or my family. I discovered that the world has so much to offer, that there are amazing people everywhere.

At least that's what I thought at the time...

INTROSPECTION

It's so likely that you have felt unseen in your life. Consider the following questions and look inside to find you – the you that deserves, and should be, in the forefront.

1. Have you ever found yourself living in the shadow of someone else's accomplishments or being unfavourably compared to others? Remember, dear friend, that you possess your own unique brilliance and potential that deserves recognition and celebration. How can you harness your own intelligence and strengths to redefine your worth and confidently step into your own spotlight?

2. Can you recall moments in your life where societal expectations and gender biases have made you feel like you didn't measure up? Embrace those experiences as opportunities for growth and empowerment. Embrace the

fact that you are more than just a comparison or societal stereotype. How can you break free from those limitations and rewrite your own narrative, forging a path that showcases your true capabilities and passions?

3. What qualities and talents do you possess that may have been overlooked or undervalued due to societal norms and expectations? Embrace them wholeheartedly and let them shine brightly. You have the power to challenge and redefine the narrow standards set for women. How can you step into the forefront and proudly showcase your uniqueness, inspiring others to do the same?

4. Reflecting on your past experiences of longing for recognition and validation, how can you shift your focus inward and recognise your own worthiness? Embrace the journey of self-discovery and self-acceptance. Embrace the truth that you are deserving of love, respect, and success just as you are. How can you cultivate self-love and confidence, knowing that you are enough, and inspire other women to do the same?

CHAPTER 2 | GROWING

"Change is never painful. Only the resistance to change is painful"
— Gautama The Lord Buddha

My experience in America was immensely transformative. Pretty much everyone in my hometown, including my parents, expected me to return after a few weeks and not see the whole year through – but I did. They all thought I was delusional when I said I would meet my celebrity crush and I did that too. I had done everything I set out to do and returned home feeling proud and accomplished. Yet no one expressed any pride in me for those accomplishments, but I didn't expect it from them. Years later I would realise that the only person who really needs to be proud of me, is me. And I'm very proud of everything I did in the States. Except maybe that silly rose tattoo on my shoulder. But hey, we all do stupid things sometimes, right?

My trip to America made me realise that I really enjoyed spending time with children and young people. I decided to study to be a preschool teacher; a career path I thought my parents wouldn't frown upon. I promised them that I would give it my all to become a successful educator. It was an opportunity to work with people, which I loved. Seeing those little humans grow into wonderful people fulfilled me on a daily basis.

As a welcome home gift, and because I needed to drive 45 minutes to the school I was enrolled in, my dad bought me my first car. It was a second-hand VW Golf 2 that was an ugly gold colour. My dad was a car mechanic so the car was always in the best mechanical condition for me to drive safely. I named it GOLDI.

I thoroughly enjoyed working to get my degree and managed to do exceptionally well. During that time, I made great friends, I learnt a lot about human behaviour and psychology, studying hard every single day. I had the opportunity to go on a two-week placement in North Germany to work with traumatised children. I loved every second of my studies! It gave me so much joy and fulfilment.

When I graduated after four years, I worked in different pre-schools, kindergarten and institutions to get the most experience in every aspect of my profession. The little town kindergarten that I went to as a child took me on for a year. Working there was like living my childhood days all over again. It still smelled the same and the little wooden chairs were still in use. So many memories from my kindergarten years came back up and I discovered how children see the world through different eyes, and learnt again to do the same. I will never forget the first day I walked through that door as an adult and not as a child. It felt like I was 5 years old again.

It made me think about how much we can learn from children and the way they see the world. I remember a situation from my own childhood – I wanted a ponytail because one of the other girls at school had one that I admired. So I asked my mum to put my hair in a ponytail for school but the minute I climbed on my kindergarten bus, I got scared and worried what the other kids would think of me, so I hid in the last row of the bus. When we arrived at school, I didn't get off with the rest of the kids and not realising that I was still there, the driver drove off to the bus base. He walked through the bus to check each row for any forgotten bags or lunch boxes and found me hiding in the last row.

All I remember after that was riding in his car back to the kindergarten. As soon as I walked in, one of the educators started yelling and telling me off – I was in massive trouble. At the time I didn't understand it and no one asked me why I didn't get off the bus. It wasn't communicated to me that they were worried about me and that was the actual reason I was in trouble. I just moved on with hiding my insecurities and doing the right thing, no matter how I felt inside.

Upon my return to the kindergarten as an adult, the director still remembered me from years back. I always wondered if they would take me on as her replacement, once she retired. I learned so much from her and wanted to keep the wonderful family-like environment alive that she created over the years. We had a very special bond, like mother and daughter. She understood me so well and we talked for hours even after a long day working with kids – about friendship, educating children and being an influence for little humans. I wanted to inspire others, too, with my work. She inspired me every day with her big heart, how she interacted with people and how she made everyone around her feel valued and loved.

One day she said to me, "Don't get stuck in this town Mel, you are meant to do great things, not here, go and explore the world, there is so much more out there for you than this small town. You are the kind of girl who can move mountains."

Never, ever settle for less than you deserve.

Those words encouraged me to leave my comfort zone. I went on to work with ADHD children, I helped with speech development and worked in an integrated community preschool, with lots of foreign families. I also started up a mum's group through the community. We met weekly where I helped foreign women with their language skills. I taught them German and guided them to better understand German culture. I loved working with migrants and helping them learn. It was an incredible group of wonderful women.

During this time, I was dating my first real boyfriend. We had met when I first returned from America. He was from a neighbouring town. He came from a big family and I really loved spending time with them. Even though I knew he wasn't the man I would marry and have a family with, I was happy enough with him. We were together for seven years until my life changed completely, one winter weekend at Karneval.

Karneval is a big celebration at the beginning of the year in Germany, where everyone dresses up and there are street parades, lots of drinking, loud music and partying in the street and all local pubs. At the time, my brother owned a car tuning club and was part of the street parade in a big truck. We had all dressed up in ugly white overalls as part of the display.

All of sudden *he* was standing there. I noticed him immediately – a tall guy with ashy long blonde hair, gorgeous from head to toe. When he smiled at me, I knew I had met the love of my life.

My friend was standing next to me, and must have noticed my instant attraction to him. She elbowed me really hard, trying to get me out of my daydream and whispered, "I think he is a bit too much for you, Mel."

It certainly was an instant attraction from both sides. We talked the whole day, and just by the way he looked at me and flirted with me, I knew it was meant to be. I had never felt that way about a guy before.

He was known as a bit of a player and my friends warned me to be careful. But to me he was the kind of man that makes you feel as if you are the only person in the world. He understood me, he saw the whole of me and gently encouraged me to be the person I truly was. He always had something nice or funny to say. He was a great communicator, which I loved. Always telling me how he felt about me and what he saw in me, he showed me a kind of love I had never experienced before. I felt as if my life were complete.

And it was, until the day he made my world come crashing down...

INTROSPECTION

Life takes us through seasons of growth, and often we don't realise that we are growing; we're wrapped up in the moments of those seasons.

1. Think back on your early adulthood and reflect on a time that you made a move towards growth and didn't give yourself credit for it at the time. Recall a moment where you took a leap of faith, stepped out of your comfort zone, or pursued a goal that you later realised had a significant impact on your personal development. What were the circumstances that led you to take that step? How did it challenge your perceptions of yourself and your capabilities? Looking back, how do you see that experience as a catalyst for growth? What strengths or qualities did you uncover within yourself during that time?

2. What did these moments of growth teach you about yourself and how did they help build your confidence in yourself? Reflect on the skills you acquired, the challenges you overcame, and the hurdles you faced during these growth experiences. How did each of these instances contribute to shaping your self-image and enhancing your self-esteem? Consider the lasting impact of recognizing your own potential and celebrating your achievements. How has this newfound confidence influenced your decisions and actions in subsequent chapters of your life?

3. Who are the people who helped you along the path to finding and building your self-awareness and confidence? Identify the mentors, friends, family members, or individuals who played a pivotal role in guiding you during your journey of personal growth. What specific qualities or insights did these individuals possess that enabled them to provide you with valuable guidance and support? Recall a significant conversation or piece of advice that one of them shared with you. How did their encouragement contribute to your self-discovery and development?

4. In times of bliss, how did you ignore warnings that you received from those around you, those who loved you and had your best interest at heart? Reflect on moments when you may have been so immersed in positive experiences that you overlooked well-intentioned advice or concerns expressed by your loved ones. What were the factors that led you to disregard these warnings? How did your youthful enthusiasm or optimism influence your decision-making process? Now that you have gained perspective and maturity, how do you view those instances differently? What lessons have you learned from not heeding these warnings that have shaped your current approach to decision-making?

5. Reflect on your personal growth journey as a whole. How has the accumulation of various experiences, challenges, and interactions contributed to your overall self-awareness and understanding of your potential? Consider the evolution of your mindset and the values that have guided your choices. How have you harnessed the power of introspection and reflection to continually learn and adapt? What practices or strategies have you incorporated to ensure that you

recognise and appreciate your growth, even in the midst of life's transitions and challenges?

6. Take a moment to express gratitude for the journey of growth you have embarked on. Recognise the courage it takes to step into the unknown, the resilience that sustains you through challenges, and the wisdom gained from both triumphs and setbacks. How has embracing growth enriched your life and brought you closer to becoming the person you aspire to be? As you reflect on your journey through the lens of this chapter, acknowledge the value of every experience, every relationship, and every moment that has shaped your path.

CHAPTER THREE | FALLING

"The soul that sees beauty may sometimes walk alone."
— Johann Wolfgang von Goethe

They say that when you meet your soulmate time stands still and that every fibre of your being tells you "this is the one". It may sound like a cliché, but I can honestly still say today that on that night, in that moment, I fell completely in love with him.

From that day on, nobody else existed for me. I ended it with my boyfriend, who really hadn't done a thing wrong. But right from the beginning this man knew how to love me. He didn't just say all the right things, he spoke to my soul. He had an adventurous spirit too and I just knew we would go places together.

We met in February and just before my birthday in May, I moved into a new apartment. He was completely involved in the move and helped me set it all up. Back then I wished that he was moving in too, and he might as well have, given the amount of time we spent together. I remember coming home from work on the day of my birthday and he had filled the apartment with 100 balloons.

Our excitement at being together was mutual. We both felt like the luckiest people alive. It really was a fairytale.

He showered me with words, always telling me that I was beautiful and skinny (something I would later come to realise was not the most positive thing.) I could tell that he was completely in love with me, and he often told me that when we first met he thought I was out of his league. In fact, he said he'd seen me driving around town and had always noticed me but never thought he'd have a chance.

He lifted me up in a way I'd never been uplifted before. He was very affectionate as well, and those things made me feel incredibly loved. He gave me all that I needed. We spent all of our spare time together and once I'd completed my personal training qualification and was working at a local gym, he really got into fitness as well and we'd exercise together. He was always there to support me, cheering me on from the sidelines.

The unconditional support was completely different from anything I'd experienced before. We spoke incessantly about our future together – having children and where we wanted to be. I'm clearly a big dreamer and have always had big goals. He was there with me and we were looking in the same direction. I had a family, a beautiful home and romantic holidays in my future – it was something we spoke about often.

Despite everyone warning me to be careful, I could see no wrong in him at all. To me, he was my prince charming. Attentive, attractive, funny, intelligent – all the things a woman could wish for. Any little warnings from friends and even my own mother were pushed away completely. He adored me.

Other women always looked at him, because he really was gorgeous and I think he enjoyed the extra acknowledgement but I certainly didn't notice him looking back. I just couldn't see him ever wanting another woman. I mean, when would he have the time? We were constantly together.

Years later he told me that a good friend of his told him that "Mel is not a one-night stand kind of girl". I was never interested in just hooking up with anyone that I didn't love or trust. I always craved meaningful relationships. Although he had a reputation for being a player, I think everyone eventually saw that we were completely committed and both in it for the long haul.

One of my close friends who I'd known since my school days, also tried to warn me about him. People said I was blind and naïve for not seeing that he was a womaniser and would break my heart. He had never been in such a long term relationship like I had before, but I just figured that he hadn't met the right girl yet. Besides, he always assured me that I was different to anyone else.

My parents were wary of him too. Maybe because he was so good-looking and confident, also a bit cocky. My mum told me that it's not all about good looks but I didn't know what she was talking about. He wasn't very kind about my family and he teased my brother a lot – about his obsession with bike riding, going to gym and working out. They were the same age and got along with each other at family gatherings, but they were never really friends. I would join in with the teasing because I really did think it was all in good fun. Years later I realised that sometimes that type of teasing can be very hurtful.

His good looks and natural confidence made him the life and soul of any party. He was almost always the centre of attention and he was mine. I'd bagged the hottest guy in town and he was sticking by me! He always dressed nicely and he washed his hair every morning and straightened his blonde ends. He had the coolest hairstyle and years later while looking at photos, we laughed about his obsession with his mane.

He always knew he was good-looking and he seemed a bit vain and arrogant about it, but that was just the outside shell that everyone else was seeing. Not me – I saw more. He was vulnerable. We spoke about everything. We were like best friends who had no secrets. It felt like it's us against the world.

He was very ambitious and worked extremely hard. He managed to fly through the ranks at whichever job he had, and was genuinely valuable to his bosses. But, he never believed he got the recognition he deserved and often complained about other people, saying they were lazy or incompetent. Of course I felt the same way – my man was magnificent and he really should get the attention and recognition he so obviously deserved.

Quite soon into our relationship he moved in with me and it got even better then. We cooked together, talked for hours and loved just being in each other's company. We watched movies, made plans for the future, took heaps of silly pictures of us together and whenever we went out, we were always within touching distance. I didn't care what anyone thought about us – I didn't care if we were that couple that makes everyone want to gag because we were so in love.

He loved food, he was into every kind of cuisine. I enjoyed cooking for him, because he was happy with anything. I'd never really enjoyed cooking before and didn't think I was really very good at it either, but cooking for him was special; and especially when we did it together.

As a child I was never much into food – I struggled to finish what was put in front of me and one of the rules at home was that we had to finish all our food. My parents always said I needed to eat more because I was too skinny. However, when I was 16 and starting putting on a bit of weight, my mum told me to stop. Once she even told me I shouldn't eat so much or I'd get fat. It was all quite contradictory. It might seem shocking in today's world, but back then, super skinny was in fashion. I do believe that she only wanted the best for me, knowing that losing weight can be extremely challenging.

Reflecting now, I realise that I was very aware of my body growing up and didn't like it much. When I entered my teens I experienced a growth spurt that caused me to have stretch marks on my thighs. I hated them and would never go to the pool with my friends and I certainly never wore short skirts or clothes that showed off my body.

I really struggled with my body and self-image. If I knew back then what I know now, I wish I hadn't stressed so much about my outside appearance. I can't imagine a single day that I was actually happy with my body, my weight or the way I looked. I never learnt to love myself in a way that I do today. No matter how the times have changed, I know that so many young women are going through struggles with their weight.

In spite of those childhood feelings of inadequacy, with him I felt like the most beautiful, sexy woman alive and my insecurities were on hold for a while. Even though I didn't notice him looking at other women, I always had this sense that I needed to make a huge effort to make sure I kept him. It was then that I really started developing strict eating habits; watching my calories, being careful about what I ate and making little rules for myself – if I had that meal, then I would skip the next one and so on. I had it completely under control, of course.

When we were together, I didn't want to disappoint him by not eating. At the same time, he always commented on my body saying that he liked the way I looked, and didn't find bigger girls attractive. This made me particularly mindful of what I ate and how much I ate. As a result, I grew to like the idea of throwing up after a big meal to stay slim.

We go out of our way to become 'perfect', but we never quite seem to get there. We put a bone-crushing amount of pressure on ourselves just to measure up to the images the media throws at us. I wish someone had told me back then that I'm beautiful the way I am. Even though he would always tell me I'm beautiful and skinny, I constantly felt the pressure to stay that way and remain slim.

When you lack confidence, that self-belief needs to be learned through experience – I am incredibly grateful and proud to have learnt it myself, through my challenges in life, going through tough times and exploring my inner beauty and worth. You can't let your mind bully your body. No matter how many stretch marks or belly rolls you have, you are beautiful and you are enough.

About six months into our relationship, he got a job offer that he couldn't refuse... in Australia. He really wanted the job, and he really wanted me so he asked me to move to Australia with him. An adventure! In another country. Of course I said yes.

INTROSPECTION

Sometimes red flags match the decor of your soul – so you miss them completely. I can't imagine there is anyone alive that hasn't ignored a red flag, or even an inkling of one. But even if you have missed a whole host of them, be kind to yourself and learn.

1. Have you ever found yourself captivated by the allure of a person or situation, only to later realise that you had missed important warning signs that were staring you right in the face? Reflect on those moments when red flags matched the decor of your soul, leading you to overlook them. How can you develop a keener sense of awareness and intuition to ensure that you don't miss those red flags in the future?

2. Can you recall a specific instance where you had a gut feeling or a subtle hint that something was amiss, but chose to

ignore it? It's a shared experience among us all, dear friend, to sometimes brush aside those inklings of red flags. How can you learn from those past instances and cultivate the courage to trust your instincts and honour those warning signs moving forward?

3. What are some common red flags that you have overlooked in the past, and what lessons have you learned from those experiences? Take a moment to reflect on the patterns and behaviours that you may have ignored or downplayed. How can you empower yourself to recognise and address those red flags head-on, prioritising your well-being and happiness?

4. In the journey of personal growth and self-awareness, how can you develop a greater sense of discernment to spot red flags, even when they blend seamlessly into your surroundings? Embrace the knowledge that we all make mistakes, and that missing red flags is a part of the human experience. How can you cultivate self-compassion and equip yourself with the tools and knowledge to navigate relationships and situations more mindfully, ensuring that your own needs and boundaries are honoured?

CHAPTER FOUR | FLYING AWAY

"Happiness is not something ready-made. It comes from your own actions."

— Dalai Lama

He left for Australia in September to begin his new job. And since I could only join him in December, it was three months of really missing each other. We had video calls every morning and every night. His loneliness was palpable over the phone. It was certainly tough for him being in a new country and adjusting to a new job in a new industry. I applied for a work and travel visa online and got all my paperwork sorted to leave Germany.

By the time I left in December 2005, I felt like I was in a movie – getting on a plane to be with my true love. Even though I had travelled before to America, and I knew I wanted to travel more and see the world, it just felt a bit unreal. I had a one-way ticket to a new life. Just me and the man of my dreams – I was excited for that!

I was ready for a new chapter and no one could ever talk me out of it. He'd really battled on his own before I arrived – he was young and alone in a foreign country. Even though he had a personality that made him instantly popular, he still battled to adjust. When I finally arrived, he looked like a lost little boy that had just been found again. I could feel it too; he lit up when he saw me and was instantly happy again.

I remember that day as if it were yesterday, I was exhausted and so overwhelmed from the 24-hour flight. He picked me up at the airport with a big welcome sign and took me straight to the beach. He felt so proud to show me our new home.

We didn't have much in the beginning and lived in a one bedroom studio right on the beach. We paid $200 rent a week, which was a lot for us and we had to really watch our spending. But it was all I needed and wanted, as long as I had him – we made a strong team. We had no TV or internet and spent our time together walking along the beach, taking a boat out, playing cards and feeding the birds on our balcony. We simply enjoyed each other in all ways.

The first week at our flat in Palm Beach

Our first Christmas together was very simple; we cooked together and gave each other little gifts. It rained for three days, but it didn't bother us at all. We stayed in our little flat and enjoyed the little things around us. I was secretly hoping he would propose to me that Christmas. When it didn't happen, I assumed that New Year's Eve would be the day. It was clear to both of us that we were meant for each other. I left my home town for him and it all just felt right. It would be so perfect. I always follow my heart and I learned over the years that if love and passion are involved, you can't go wrong. NEVER.

Christmas in Australia

He worked for an incredibly successful small business and his boss and his wife became our closest friends. In fact, I'm still friends with them today. They looked after us so well and helped us in every way possible to get comfortable. They had some friends that owned a house near the city and invited us to stay there with them over New

Year's Eve. I was so excited to see the Sydney fireworks and couldn't wait to spend that special time with him, it all still felt like a dream.

In Australia there are two fireworks sessions: one at 9pm (for families with kids) and one at midnight. They are both spectacular and especially in Sydney, the NYE fireworks are incredible. We headed to the city super early that day, trying to get a good spot, but everything was already taken, and we couldn't get into any restaurant or bar - there simply wasn't space anywhere. The entire city seemed to be out and about for the show.

By the time the 9pm fireworks were about to start I was starving. I hadn't eaten all day, because I wanted to look great in my dress in case he did propose (how silly, I know). I also thought we would have a romantic dinner somewhere at a restaurant. I started to feel a weird sensation overcoming me. The combination of being hungry and dehydrated with the hot and humid weather, that I was still adjusting to, and possibly jet lag was hitting me too. My head was spinning, my legs started to shake and I became weak, all while we were trying to get through the crowds to see the fireworks. I knew I was going to pass out.

The next minute I woke up lying on the floor with my legs up and about twenty people around me. I heard him saying, "No, she is ok, she's not used to the heat, she just needs some water." And the first thing I thought was, "Shit, I ruined the proposal!"

He insisted on going back to the house, but I assured him I was fine, and we decided to walk back closer to home, away from the crowds. On the way, we discovered a little hiding spot, where you could have a peek at the bridge and see the fireworks. It was perfect. We sat down at a little bench and watched the rest of the 9pm fireworks which went on for quite a while.

Even though I still felt weak and exhausted, it was the perfect moment. Watching the fireworks with the man I wanted to share my life with was simply magical. That's when it happened – the moment I had been dreaming about since the day I spotted him at Karneval. He pulled out a gorgeous ring and finally popped the question. And of course I said "YES!"

His job kept him busy so I looked into getting a job as a nanny. It was something that I was way over qualified for, but it was a great way to start so that I could enjoy being in my new homeland as much as possible without too much responsibility. And I really wanted to be able to spend as much time as possible with my fiancée, exploring the city and finding our way together. I also needed to get all my qualifications assessed to be recognised in Australia as an experienced and qualified teacher. Even after improving my English a lot in America – watching Disney movies and TV shows with the kids – it still wasn't good enough to be able to work at a preschool straight away.

I made friends quickly, ready to re-create my whole new life Down Under. It was an interesting time for me because I could just be me. Back home, everyone had a version of me in their head, and it didn't matter who I really was, they believed they knew me. But in Australia, nobody knew me and anyone I met would simply take me as I presented myself. I immediately became super close with his boss' wife. She welcomed us so warmly to Australia and spent a lot of time with me, helping me find my feet. She is one of a kind; I've never met anyone with such a big heart. She really looked after me, picked me up when he was working, so I wouldn't be alone. She took me shopping and showed me around. We forged a very strong bond.

Before leaving for Australia, I'd connected with a few families with the view of being a nanny for the first few months to help me get my bearings. I visited a few of the families, but nothing was really so close that I could walk from the place where we lived at the time. Since I didn't have a car, I needed something super close by or aligned with his working hours, so that he could drop me off before work and pick me up afterwards.

It didn't take long to find a lovely family in the next suburb, they had three children and a beautiful house. I will never forget the day I visited them for my first interview. Being German, of course I arrived nicely dressed and way too early and with all my paperwork and qualifications in a big folder. No one would have been able to read it in my mother language, but I thought I'd take it anyway – to impress, of course. I really wanted the job, so I could help with our expenses.

The house was near the beach in *Avalon*, and when I got to the front door it was open. I knocked anyway and I could hear kids' voices, music and the sound of the birds. Australia has that special sound to it – consistent birdsong. I think at that moment I fell in love with the area. It was just the perfect spot. It was quiet, no tourists, lots of great cafes and cute boutiques, lots of playgrounds, parks, palm trees and the beach was just stunning. So untouched, so natural, so clear. Still today this place holds a special place in my heart. We also named our first born after it – *Lui Avalon*.

I slowly walked up the stairs and said 'hellooooo'. I walked through the big open kitchen area and saw two kids playing on the floor. They smiled at me. Silvia walked in from another room and said "You must be Melanie, sorry I didn't hear you coming in ". She was carrying a nine-month-old little boy. Before she could say anything else, her phone rang and she put the baby down on the floor and answered the call. The boy started to crawl up to her and cried. I picked him up, distracted him and sat down with the other two kids. I instantly felt a connection with this family. I met her husband Travis and we sat down for an interview where they asked me thousands of questions. Years later they confessed that the minute I walked in and picked up little baby Ian, they had decided to hire me.

I started working there the very next day and I instantly felt like I was a part of their family. It reminded me of my time in America. The Australian lifestyle was so relaxed and laid back. I struggled with my German mindset, but Travis always cracked a joke about the Germans to lighten my mood. I discovered that our culture was considered very stiff and a lot of people admired us for our hard working nature.

Being a nanny had its ups and downs but Silvia and Travis were incredible people and made it a wonderful experience. Silvia worked at a big computer company and Travis was an entrepreneur who worked from home. They were the most laid-back and down-to-earth individuals, making me feel welcome from the start. I was completely integrated into their family and it was so refreshing to experience a secure family life, knowing these could be friends for life. And they indeed still are.

I learned so much working full-time for Silvia and Travis. I treated their children like they were my own. Lizzy and Bob attended Montessori, and I drove them to school in the family car. Throughout the day, I cared for little Ian, taking him to the playground and the beach, interacting with other mothers, and later picking up the older two. Silvia and Travis had demanding jobs, which often resulted in me working long hours. I felt like a stay-at-home mum, handling laundry, cleaning, preparing meals, and playing with the children – essentially all the responsibilities of a mother. I engaged the children in various activities, such as arts and crafts. They even took me on weekend outings, further solidifying our bond.

Travis was one of the funniest guys ever, we formed a special bond, like a father-daughter, or brother-sister type bond. We joked around a lot and he always laughed about my sense of fashion and commitment to food and exercise, in a caring kind of way, of course. However, I always looked forward to the moments when my dream man picked me up.

At times I felt overwhelmed, and longed for adult interaction. I eventually had a conversation with Silvia and Travis about my feelings, and they responded by offering me a raise, even though they knew I couldn't remain their nanny forever. They were immensely helpful to me in assisting with getting my German qualifications assessed in Australia and when they were finally all done, I was able to apply for a job at a child-care centre.

Working in an environment that involved adults too was a much-needed change of pace for me. I formed meaningful friendships and gained insights into the Australian education system, discovering huge differences in curriculum and regulations.

My English got better every week and I even started to dream and think in English. Despite feeling overqualified for my position, I remained dedicated to the children, passionate about teaching them the right things and fostering their optimal development.

However, I soon grew frustrated as I lacked the authority to effect meaningful change. Sydney's Northern Beaches had numerous child care centres, each with its own approach. My desire to transform the industry or take on a more senior role was growing each day. I was frustrated; I wanted to educate those children and bring across my knowledge. There was so much more we could do to help those little humans and families.

We had been in Australia for three years when my parents came to visit for the first time in 2009. We were living in Narrabeen at the time, in a place directly on the beach with a beautiful view. I was working at a local child care centre as an assistant and asked for a week off, but they declined. I was devastated; I needed to be with my parents and show them around. They didn't speak a word of English so I needed to be there and spend time with them. I appreciated the effort they put into the trip so much, considering that they weren't interested in travelling at all. They had just flown twenty-four hours to see me. I went all or nothing and said if I'm not getting a week off work, I had to resign. So I did, for my parents. Of course I didn't tell them that I just resigned from my job. I didn't want them to worry, but I knew I would find something else soon. I knew it.

I applied for a director's role at a preschool during the time my parents were visiting us. I prayed every day that they would call me for an interview. My mum and dad asked about my job and I just couldn't tell them that I resigned because of them. So I pretended everything was fine. I will never forget the day when I got the phone call and I was asked to come in for an interview. When the call came in, we were all dressed up as Chinese people in the middle of a Chinese garden in Sydney. I was so excited and my mood instantly changed from pretending to be happy to "OMG, I can achieve anything!"

I negotiated a salary that exceeded the average for such a position, unaware that I would need to rebuild the school from scratch. It became my personal project, and I adored the challenge it presented. I was the first one there in the morning, arriving at 7am after a thirty minute drive, and often the last to leave around six or 7pm. Most days I worked twelve hour shifts, pouring my heart and soul into the preschool's success. Gradually, it became one of the most reputable establishments in the area.

It felt like my own child, and I remained responsible for enrolling and training staff, ensuring that we surpassed ordinary standards for everyone involved. I took great pride in the high accreditation results we achieved, and the children who attended our school consistently excelled. The owner of the preschool provided unwavering support and care. She nurtured our relationship, regularly bringing me coffee, treating me to lunch, and even buying baby clothes when I was pregnant with my first child years later. She organised fantastic staff dinners and never failed to surprise us with presents and treats. Working there brought me immense joy. I still visited Silvia and Travis and the kids on a weekly basis. I was still part of their family and I loved Lizzy, Bob and Ian as if they were my own children.

Of course, running the preschool came with its share of staffing challenges. We went through several employees as they struggled to meet the workload. I had high expectations, aiming only for the best of the best, training them to deliver exceptional care to both the children and their parents. Our dedication paid off as we achieved the highest assessment grades, with all the children demonstrating remarkable advancement. I took tremendous pride in these accomplishments.

I wanted to create a team that was like a family. Women who can work together and support each other can accomplish so much. I put my heart and soul into it and I wanted to build a community and sisterhood without any drama, negativity, or jealousy; just pure fun, educational support and engaging strong work efforts.

Working with people, especially with children and women, has always fulfilled me. Teaching children and helping them grow into strong personalities was something that I felt was my calling.

I got into exercising more and more, getting up at 5am to go for a run before work. My days were so busy at the preschool that I survived on only two large coffees and water. By the time I'd get home in the evenings I would be so hungry that I felt sick and nauseous. I'd eat everything I could and then feel guilty for making such unhealthy food choices. I'd feel like a failure for losing control after a 'good' day and immediately purge everything I had just eaten. By now, my eating disorder was in full swing.

We both quickly started to earn more money and we were able to upgrade to a new car and move to a different place. We loved living at the Northern Beaches and enjoyed long beach walks in the morning, strolling the local markets and decorating our new place. I made really good friends with some of the girls at my work and Australia became more and more my home. We flew to Germany once a year to see our families, but it always felt so good to leave again after a few weeks. We realised with every visit that Germany was not the country we wanted to live in anymore and neither would we consider it a country to raise our children in the future.

A year after we got engaged, a friend from Germany stayed with us for a few weeks. She was travelling through the country and stopped by to visit us. We spent Christmas with her and I remember so clearly sitting on our beautiful balcony in an extraordinary penthouse style apartment in Mona Vale, in one of the most prestigious areas. It was a warm summer night, I had a red and white striped t-shirt dress on, which I loved and felt so pretty in. I can still smell the perfume I got for Christmas that year. We took lots of pictures, had a few drinks. The three of us laughed and had great conversations. I felt so proud to accommodate people from our home town, show them around and help them get to know the country. And I was so proud of us as a couple for sticking together and being the happiest we've ever been.

At least that's what I thought. In a split second everything changed...

He went to the bathroom and his mobile phone went off a couple of times. I was in a conversation with our friend but because the phone didn't stop beeping, I picked it up. As I glanced at the phone, I saw a message pop up from a girl and it said, 'I want to kiss you right now, too'. The text was in German, so I knew she wasn't from Australia.

My heart dropped, I felt this immense pain in my chest and I felt like throwing up. My hands were shaking, but I calmly put the phone back on the table and pretended I needed the bathroom. I didn't want our friend to see what I just saw.

He was just returning from the bathroom and I asked him to come with me. We went downstairs to the guest bathroom and I fell on the floor, crying, shaking and completely heartbroken. He knew exactly what I was talking about and said that there was nothing going on between him and her and it was just simply one message and nothing to worry about.

My night was ruined, but I got myself together and told him that I was going back to Germany in the morning. I walked back up to our friend and pretended that nothing happened. As I was walking back with a fake smile on my face, she asked when the big wedding would finally be. It was like pouring salt in the wound.

My self-esteem crashed big time after that text. I was so sure about this man and his love for me. But now I wasn't entirely sure anymore. He tried hard to convince me to stay, and told me that nothing had happened with this girl. I questioned everything in my mind – why wasn't I enough for him? I truly loved him and tried so hard to make him happy. My body issues and insecurities started to creep in again, and I went from purging about twice a week to pretty much everyday. To ensure that I didn't get too skinny, I would always eat something healthy afterwards – it became an exhausting cycle.

I refused to even ask questions because it hurt me too much. I wanted to brush the whole thing under the carpet and just forget. But that was easier said than done. The next three months turned out to be quite challenging. I didn't tell any of my girlfriends about it; I felt so embarrassed. So I went on with my life with him and tried to deal with it alone.

For me messaging someone else is cheating and I truly believe that when you love someone you wouldn't be interested in kissing or reaching out to anybody. Back then I was still naïve; I loved him more than anything and believed every word he said. Every night I fell asleep in agony at the thought of him wanting to kiss another girl. It took about six months for me to fully get over it. We never spoke about it again and I decided never to ask any questions. I just wanted to forget. The pain lessened over the years, until it faded away. Or so I thought…

We travelled a lot - going on loads of cruises, and travelled to Asia, New Zealand and around Australia. We visited all the places we always wanted to go to and still managed to fly to Germany to see family yearly. One of my most memorable experiences was doing a beach skydive. Overcoming that fear and being scared but doing it anyway, is something that I would continue doing throughout my life. That feeling of free-falling and then landing with an incredible amount of pride, was priceless.

Jumping out of the plane for my beach skydive

My brother and his girlfriend came to visit twice and when they got married and had a baby in 2010, I really felt the urge to become a mum too. Holding my little baby nephew during a stay in Germany was incredible. I loved babies and children, but that love was next level.

We had talked about having children a few times and I was ready when I turned 30. It was a big turning point for me. Everyone around me already had kids or was pregnant. I saw babies and pregnant women everywhere. I also knew that as soon as I got pregnant I would have to finally stop all my damaging eating habits.

However, at that time my bulimic habits were starting to show – my hair was thinning and I suffered from terrible stomach cramps and I was tired all the time. I was so unhealthy. I knew that as soon as there was a baby growing inside of me, I would need to be the healthiest I could be.

In February 2011 I fell pregnant and felt that my life just couldn't get any better. I was so excited and couldn't believe my luck. I was going to be a mummy. But at eight weeks, I lost the baby. I'll never forget that night – he was away on a business trip and I had bought my friend, Tamara tickets to a Katy Perry concert for her birthday.

It was Saturday night and the day before I'd told the team at work that I was going to have a baby. I was so proud and couldn't wait any longer to tell everyone. I was in the shower getting ready for our girls night out when I started bleeding. I immediately knew something was wrong and took myself to a nearby clinic for an ultrasound.

They found that I had a blighted ovum. It's where the early embryo never develops or stops developing and is reabsorbed, leaving an empty gestational sac. I was assured this didn't mean anything horrendous and that I could easily go on to have another viable pregnancy. Regardless, it was still really hard. They told me that I would miscarry in the next day or so.

I felt so heartbroken, why would this happen to me?

Tamara came over with wine and sushi and all the treats I couldn't have while I was pregnant and we spent the evening together. crying. She tried to calm me down, distract me as much as possible, but that evening my heart bled. I miscarried the following Monday.

I took a week off work and cried for five days straight. I doubted my body was capable of having a child and I blamed myself because of my strict and harmful eating habits, even though I stopped purging the moment I found out I was pregnant. I also made sure that I was getting everything the baby needed for a healthy pregnancy. My doctor assured me that I could try getting pregnant again within my next cycle. So I kept focussing on my body's signal to indicate ovulation and the right time to try again.

I felt that talking openly about miscarrying would help me overcome the grief. When you lose your baby, you think you are the only person going through that type of pain and loss, but in fact, not many people talk openly about miscarriage and a lot are probably even unnoticed. So many times we are told to just move on and try getting pregnant again quickly. But it is a very real loss and women should be allowed the time they need to grieve.

My fiancée was a great support, holding me and crying with me. He had also lost a child – we forget sometimes that men are also invested in the new life that we women carry. He couldn't have been more gentle and supportive and I was so grateful to have him with me. Yet, I still felt low and disappointed. I felt like I wasn't enough and a few weeks after the miscarriage, I started purging my food again. It seemed like a never-ending cycle.

Not long after the miscarriage, I fortunately fell pregnant again. I immediately got back into healthy eating habits and despite my anxiety, the pregnancy was viable. I continued working at the school until the end of the year and we decided to get married in the coming weeks and return to Germany for good to give birth in our home country. We only had a temporary Visa for Australia and giving birth here would have cost us an arm and a leg. Knowing that we would be completely taken care of in Germany, made the decision a no-brainer.

After our six-year engagement, we decided to get married before heading back to Germany and having our baby. We always wanted to be married before we had children, so it was the perfect time. Since we loved cruising, we decided to take a two week cruise through the South Pacific Islands as a final holiday in Australia. It was the perfect place to have a very low-key wedding since we didn't want to get married in Australia away from our families, or get married in Germany away from our friends. I liked that we chose to have a very intimate wedding without any guests.

I went wedding dress shopping with a few of my girlfriends at one of the most prestigious wedding stores. I found a super gorgeous dress that my girlfriends talked me into buying. But two weeks before the wedding, I had changed my mind and I just didn't like it anymore. I tried to sell it, which was an inconvenience at the time. It turns out that it's quite challenging to sell a second-hand couture dress. I ended up ordering a different dress online from an American website that only cost a third of the designer dress. I fell in love with it and I still have it today.

The whole wedding was inexpensive too. I organised everything. We had a photographer from the island who offered a lovely wedding package. They picked us up from the ship and took us to the spot where we had the ceremony. It was all so beautiful – they put up a big lapa decorated with flowers and pebbles. They organised a cake for us too. I did my makeup myself and had a hairdresser do my hair earlier on the ship. It had rained and was so humid that the beautiful curls didn't last but I didn't mind. My favourite part was my wedding dress. I had someone help me get into it before the ceremony.

Our wedding on the cruise ship

It was such a cute and intimate ceremony – everything we could have hoped for. Afterwards, we had a romantic meal before getting back on the ship in our wedding outfits. One of the restaurants on the ship had also made up a cake for us. One of the guests we'd met on the ship was a photographer and he took some photos for us too and sent them to us later for free. We ended up with heaps of photos to remember that special day. It was everything I had dreamed about and all I could have wanted for a wedding day. The wedding was halfway through the cruise so we had another week to celebrate our honeymoon and spend time together just the two of us before baby Lui arrived and made us a family of three.

Once we returned from our wedding cruise, we started preparing to go back to Germany. It was bittersweet leaving the preschool I had transformed into a thriving and sought-after institution. The school felt like family, and I departed with a heavy heart, knowing that I had left behind a really special place. We had breathed new life into an old building, turning it into an incredible school—a testament to our dedication and passion. The girls organised a baby shower for me which was my farewell party too.

My preschool team

We'd been in Sydney for six years and I really felt like a completely different person. Not just because we'd found a home in Australia, but because I could finally be myself, live my dreams; I felt free and rooted. While going back to Germany made sense because of my pregnancy, it wasn't going to be easy leaving a place I'd really come to love as my home.

Our last Christmas in Australia, pregnant with Lui

INTROSPECTION

Reinventing yourself is a powerful and freeing thing. It's not often that we get that chance, but I urge you to take it if you can. If you are in the process of reinvention, have already done it, or want to, consider the following questions.

1. Imagine embarking on a new chapter of your life, whether it be moving to a new place or experiencing a life-altering event. How does this fresh start provide you with the opportunity to redefine yourself and step into the person you have always aspired to be?

2. In this moment of reinvention, what aspects of your identity and personality do you wish to shed, and what new qualities and traits do you envision embracing? Embrace the freedom to rewrite the script of your life and intentionally craft the person you desire to become.

3. Reflecting on past experiences, what are the lessons you have learned and the insights you have gained that can guide your reinvention? How can you harness the wisdom gained from your journey to shape a new narrative for yourself, filled with authenticity, growth, and fulfilment?

4. As you embark on this transformative journey of reinvention, how can you create a supportive environment that fosters your growth and nurtures your newfound identity? Surround

yourself with individuals who inspire and uplift you, and seek out opportunities that align with your aspirations. How can you manifest your dreams and embrace the freedom to be the best version of yourself in this new chapter of your life?

CHAPTER FIVE | FLYING BACKWARDS

"Women are the real architects of society. They have the power to build, nurture, and transform."
— Harriet Beecher Stowe

Going back to Germany was heartbreaking. I had felt so much more at home in Sydney than I ever had in Germany - the weather, the people, the beaches, the lifestyle. I was grateful for it every single day and just thinking about Germany made me feel cold. And empty.

I'd been able to be myself completely in Australia and going back, I knew that the old fears and insecurities would come flooding back. I had terrible back pain for the two weeks before we flew back and I'm sure some of the pain was caused by stress. I spent most of the time hanging in the pool at Travis and Silvia's house, as I couldn't stand up, sit or lay down at all. I wondered how I would survive a 24-hour flight back home.

Pregnant with Lui, a week before returning to Germany

My husband was in his element, though. He was tired of his job in Sydney and had managed to get a job at a company he'd always wanted to work for back in Germany. So, for him, he was flying towards his dream. I was flying back to a place where I didn't feel like I belonged anymore. I had never envisioned living a family life in

Germany. I just could not see it happening after all those years in Australia.

My parents were over the moon, of course. We arrived back to a huge welcome home sign that my old girlfriends had organised, and five of my closest friends were there - all keen to see my big belly. It was a lovely homecoming, even though it was one of the coldest winters in over thirty years. Coming from thirty-five degree heat and humidity to minus-twenty was pretty tough to adjust to.

At first, we moved into my old bedroom at my parents' house, which really wasn't ideal. I hadn't lived at home for many years, so going back there evoked a multitude of strange feelings and misgivings. As a pregnant couple, it wasn't easy to find a rental, so we didn't really have a choice. He didn't like the idea of moving in with my parents either and I just knew that this would be a very conflicting time for all of us.

The only thing that made me feel good being home was that everyone else was happy and for once I felt that I wasn't a disappointment to anyone. Along with feeling my baby in my growing belly. I loved being pregnant! I've never felt so feminine, so sensual and womanly before. Carrying a baby brought out the best in me. For once I wasn't worried about my weight or a flat tummy. I showed it off and felt complete. And I finally got some boobs too, which I wasn't blessed with before.

My husband dove right into his job and instantly he was hardly ever home. I remember sleeping quite a lot and while I was tired from the pregnancy, I think I was also quite depressed – it felt like I'd gone backwards. Even though I was enjoying feeling the life growing inside me and was excited about finally becoming a mum, it was hard to adjust. I was pretty bored and lonely during that time, even though everyone fussed over me. I could feel how relieved my mum was that we were finally back home. My mum was cooking for me and it was probably a good thing that she did. It helped me to eat more robust meals and stay healthy during my pregnancy. I had no desire to purge at all while pregnant. In fact, I felt the best I ever had about my health and my body when I was pregnant.

My back was still not 100%, but I could at least move around without massive pain. I missed the warm weather and relaxing in the pool so I signed up for an Aqua pregnancy class at the local indoor pool. I actually got a bit excited to hopefully meet some other mums.

The Aqua class became the highlight of my week. Maybe because it was the closest I could get to a beach feeling in frigid Germany. It was the only day I actually got out and did something other than waiting for my man to come home from work. There I met Tina who was due to have a baby girl around the same time as me. She invited me over to her house for coffee and we got along really well. She had just moved to the area and after being away for six years, we were both so happy to finally make some connections. I felt like I was disconnected from a lot of my old friends when we returned.

It took us six weeks to find our own place, just two weeks before my baby Lui was born. Our new home was a thirty-minute drive from my family, but I was completely fine with that because by then I really needed my own space. I needed to breathe. A very good friend that I'd met when I worked in childcare was an incredible help during that time. She was amazing with helping me set up Lui's bedroom, decorating our home and she always made me laugh. By then I was really feeling the effects of being pregnant and my belly looked like it would burst. We actually asked her to be Lui's godmother when he was born.

I was in labour for more than sixteen hours and I thought this baby would never come out. I chose a hospital further away, because I really wanted an all-natural water birth. I also refused any medication or painkillers during contractions and birth. I wanted to do this all natural and on my own, without any outside help. I wanted to have a strong feeling of empowerment during labour and a sense of accomplishment afterward. I also strongly believed that if you give birth naturally, the bond with your child is closer. Mothers are the strongest humans out there and I was ready to step into this new role, so I needed to feel this healthy pain to have a strong start in my motherhood journey. In order to have a natural birth, I needed to leave the bathtub after six hours and finally he was born after I had passed out twice and couldn't remember my name.

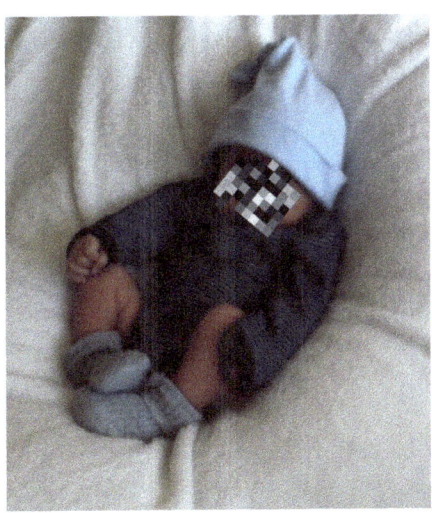

One day old Lui

Baby Lui Avalon

Lui Avalon was a tiny baby, with striking black hair and probably the reason for the intense heartburn I experienced with his pregnancy. We named him after the suburb of Avalon in Australia where we had once lived. He looked like one of those stuffed monkey Monchhichi dolls, the cutest thing ever. Naturally, everyone fell in love with him right away – my mum just couldn't get enough and my dad had the most precious bond with him from the day he was born.

The day we left the hospital I felt so scared, but the midwives told me that I had nothing to worry about – with the milk I was producing I could feed the whole hospital! I was just so scared I would not be able to breastfeed properly. I wanted to stay there and get all the help from the nurses and midwives, who were so supportive and helpful.

Despite having such a precious little thing – a tiny baby that I had always wanted so desperately – I felt completely overwhelmed and couldn't understand how everyone else was so calm around him. I didn't speak to anyone about how I was feeling because I felt like it was me that was failing. I had no idea what postpartum depression was and just did my best to get over it. I did, eventually, but those first months were very tough - with little support from family, and my husband at work most of the time. He was always happy and smiling when he came home from work while I just felt exhausted and run down. Not to mention the lack of sleep that did not help with my mood either.

My body pretty much bounced back straight away. I had only put on fifteen kilograms during my pregnancy and straight after birth I lost ten kilograms, even though Lui was only just over three kilograms. I was so pleased with this. I bought a post pregnancy tummy belt and wore it every day after giving birth to make sure my tummy would go back to how it was before pregnancy. I was also happy that I had recovered from the bulimia. I do believe that I would have crashed completely if I had to navigate the postpartum depression in conjunction with my eating disorder. I actually felt relieved that I was able to overcome this by myself and not burden anyone else with it. People say it takes nine months to grow a baby and nine months for your body to go back to what it was before. So that was my goal.

Lui was a tough baby - he wouldn't latch on and so breastfeeding became impossible. I didn't admit it at the time, but I struggled inside a lot with this. I'd tried to ensure that everything I did for the pregnancy was by the book. Literally, by every single book on pregnancy I could get my hands on. When I couldn't breastfeed, I was devastated. No one tells you that breastfeeding is something that needs to be practised. From all the books and advice I received, breastfeeding was the loveliest and easiest, most natural thing. It really isn't in the beginning. It was only years later when I had my second child, that I could experience easy breastfeeding, after struggling with Lui for three months.

Napping with Lui

I started running again eight weeks after giving birth, even though my midwife told me not to. But I needed some time for myself and running became my sanity. Our nights were long and exhausting, Lui seemed to be constantly hungry and I got more and more stressed not being able to feed him properly. So many nights I fell asleep next to his little cot, holding his hand and singing him songs.

We were living on just one income, which was paying all the bills, but it did stifle my independence. This was such a new journey for me, not being able to contribute to our family expenses. It never sat right with me. I started up at a mum's group, which did me the world of good. Tina and I met up with our little ones on a weekly basis and we saw each other at least three times a week for a coffee and baby talk.

I made new friends and found that speaking to the other mums about their lives was good for me. I still never spoke to anyone about my depression, but it slowly lifted. I've never been good at asking for help and I was sure that I could go through this on my own. I started getting used to the life we now had back in Germany, and making new friends. But I still really missed Australia, the sunshine and the beaches. Now, my days were filled with changing nappies, baby formula, nappy rashes, sleep routines and teething.

When Lui was about a year old, he wasn't sleeping through the night. I remember posting a status on Facebook the week before Christmas saying: "'All I want for Christmas is five hours of solid sleep". It was the first time I ever opened up and admitted I was struggling, in my own way of course. Being sleep deprived was something I've never experienced before and it drove me mad. To a point where I didn't want to go to sleep at night anymore, knowing that I had just one hour and then would have to get up again to feed and comfort Lui. No one could comfort him, even though I wasn't breastfeeding anymore and had switched to formula, I could not leave the house for longer than an hour.

Longing for Australia, all I could think about was all those cute beach-style clothes for kids that we couldn't get anywhere in Germany. So, I took things into my own hands. We renovated the basement of our house and I transformed it into a kids clothing store. I started researching cute children's clothes and imported them from overseas. It was just a small business but I felt so good contributing to our income. What I liked most about it was the fact that I could do this all from home and invite mums from the area to bring their little ones and do some shopping in our cute store downstairs. Lui was always dressed in the coolest and cutest outfits and everywhere we went he stood out.

The business went really well, so we decided to rent out a store in the city to get more walk-in customers. I had this great vision of inviting mums to sit down in the store, enjoy some coffee and tea, while shopping and have a cute play area for the kids to make this experience even more pleasant for new mums.

The mum's group catch-up became my new sanity. I felt like these women understood me and the challenges that came with having a baby. The mums all supported my new kid's fashion business and they loved coming by to see what was new in store. I sometimes brought the latest arrivals to our weekly catch up and we dressed the kids for a little runway show. Tina and I were there every week and we had a few new mums come along as well. Around this time, I reconnected with Stephanie, who had been at the disco my brother and I hosted at our house as teenagers. By now, she was also a mother and we bonded over our motherhood roles and being a first-time mum. The three of us became really good friends, catching up regularly, drinking coffee and sharing the new finds that made being a mum easier - from baby snacks to advice.

With her long, dark hair and deep brown eyes, Stephanie had always been the most stunning girl. I always admired her beautiful, luscious hair. It was so lovely to see her again and forge a new bond. We spoke a lot about the times when we were young and free and now stuck in motherhood with husbands and responsibilities.

When we'd moved back to Germany, none of my friends were new mothers - they'd either already had children or didn't have any at all. None were pregnant, so having a friend that I could share all the baby things with was a delight. Especially as Lui was still quite difficult – he was clingy and cried a lot. This wasn't something my mum was very supportive about; I felt like she disapproved of my clingy baby, or perhaps it was me she disapproved of? Years later I saw this situation all differently and that I may have understood her all wrong. She was possibly wrestling with her own feelings of not being enough as a mother, just like I was now. All she ever wanted was to give love.

Stephanie and I became very close and I eventually felt safe enough to open up to her and tell her about all my fears of not being a good enough mother. I shared about my struggles with breastfeeding and the depression; that I felt guilty for not being as happy as I should be with my beautiful bundle of joy in my life. She was incredibly supportive and I felt safe with her. Our weekly catch up turned into a strong friendship and I couldn't imagine life without her in it anymore.

My husband was working all the time, and I would hang out with Lui and my mum friends. I spent time decorating the shop and picking the latest fashion for those little ones. I was hosting mums' nights at our house, shopping, sipping on cranberry juice and talking about outfits for our kids and the struggles of motherhood. I also started up a little jewellery line for the mums to purchase when they came in, which turned out to be a big hit. When you become a mother, everything becomes about your child, you totally forget about spoiling yourself and don't spend money on yourself anymore. I wanted to change that mentality. I wanted those women to come into the store and feel empowered and beautiful. I wanted to make their life as mums a little easier and enable them to connect with a powerful community.

Women carry so much and becoming a mother is the toughest gig. I was in the middle of it all and when you share your challenges, feelings and emotions with each other, it feels like you are not alone. Connecting with like-minded women became my safe space, I really felt the power of us, and the power of our sisterhood.

Those friendships meant the world to me and I learned so much from them. I've always felt safer and more empowered when I have a group of women around me. I know that I wouldn't have been able to cope with my postpartum depression, the overwhelming situation as a new mum or recovering from bulimia without them.

Even though I had created so much again here in Germany, my mind constantly pulled me back to Australia. Despite building a strong mother's community, reconnecting with Stephanie, and developing new friendship with Tina, I longed for the life we had made in the sunshine, far away from all of this. My life had changed so much and I guess I just had to get on with it.

In 2013, when Lui was almost two, we had an incredible holiday; we met up with my husband's former boss and his wife, our dear friends from Sydney. We met for New Year's Eve in Paris. They also brought their son, who was almost four at the time. It was such an amazing experience for me, because I had always wanted to go to Paris. I had forgotten how much I enjoyed spending time with them and I really missed it. I was secretly hoping they had another job opportunity for him so that we could move back to Australia.

I hadn't ever mentioned my desire to go back to Australia to my husband, because I didn't want to upset him or make him feel like it was his fault that we were living a different life in Germany. I hoped he would just feel my pain and see that I wasn't happy with our current situation. As I had learned in my childhood, I continued to hide my feelings because I wanted to be the most supportive wife and mother I could be. But inside, it all felt different.

I knew that he would agree to another job offer, because he complained pretty much all day about Germany, how hard it was to get on your feet, how stupid people were and how uneducated and immature everyone was around us. Nothing had changed.

I don't think it was immaturity; the way I saw it, it was simply because we had experienced a completely different lifestyle, we had been through a lot together and we had grown together, travelled the world, stuck together when others were giving up, moved around, said goodbye many times and made new friends everywhere we went. We relied on each other, because we didn't have anyone else. While everyone else was back home in Germany, we were growing and developing big time overseas.

When I fell pregnant with Lui, it was completely planned. I did all the right things to ensure that my body was ready for a pregnancy. So, I didn't ever take precautions because I was in touch with my body and knew exactly when I was ovulating and where I was in my cycle. Well, you probably know where this is going.

It was New Year in Paris, and we were having a wonderful time with good friends. And then they asked that life-changing question: would we come back to Australia?

It was an amazing night - and that's when our youngest, Levi was made. He was born in September 2014, and we were raring to go back to Australia.

INTROSPECTION

It's interesting how we can change as much as we like but when we go back to a place where we grew up, or even to our own families, that change is not very often recognised. It's hard to maintain your new-found 'you' in such circumstances.

1. Imagine returning to a place where nobody can see the changes and progress you've made in your life. How does this opportunity to revisit your past environment impact your sense of self and the reinvention process? How does it feel to have the chance to reintroduce yourself to a familiar setting?

2. In the midst of reinventing yourself, how do you navigate the perception of your family, who have always known you in a certain way? How can you reconcile their perception with the changes you've undergone, and what strategies can you employ to communicate your growth and transformation to them effectively?

3. Reflecting on your journey of reinvention, how do you envision your family's perception of you? Will they continue to see you as they have always perceived you, or do you believe they will acknowledge and embrace the changes you've made? How does their perception influence your motivation and determination to reinvent yourself?

4. As you return to a place where nobody can witness your personal progress, how do you maintain the momentum of your reinvention? How can you stay true to the person you've become, even when others are unaware of the growth you've experienced? How does your internal validation play a role in this process?

CHAPTER SIX | FLYING HIGH

"People begin to become successful the minute they decide to be."
– Harvey MacKay

Finding out that we were having a baby again and making the decision to leave Germany after three years was intense but amazing. We spent the following nine months sorting out our visa, accommodation, getting our stuff shipped back to Australia; telling family and friends and trying not to feel guilty about making our decision. And on top of all those logistical and organisational things, we tried to continue with our life as parents, doing our best to not disrupt Lui's routine while also caring for the little boy inside my belly.

Tina was also pregnant and we started our Aqua class again together. Stephanie was devastated that we were leaving and we cried a lot together and promised each other that our friendship would never suffer, no matter the distance.

We spent those nine months sitting on packed boxes; I wore the same leggings and shirts for most of my pregnancy, which was a challenge for me. But we needed to be prepared for our visa to come through and be ready for departure.

We had cancelled our rental contract, thinking the visa would go through in three months so we needed to find a place to live for another couple of months. I would hide my belly when we went house hunting. Who would take on a family with a toddler and a pregnant wife for just three months? We were sure that THIS was the last move we had ahead of us, as nothing is more stressful than moving halfway around the globe with two kids to start up a new life again.

We finally got our visa approved, after our little Levi Ayden was born that September. I had a natural birth again and refused all kinds of medication and painkillers during labour. Levi was in a breech position most of the pregnancy and it was a wonder he turned around in time, to make this birth as natural as it could be.

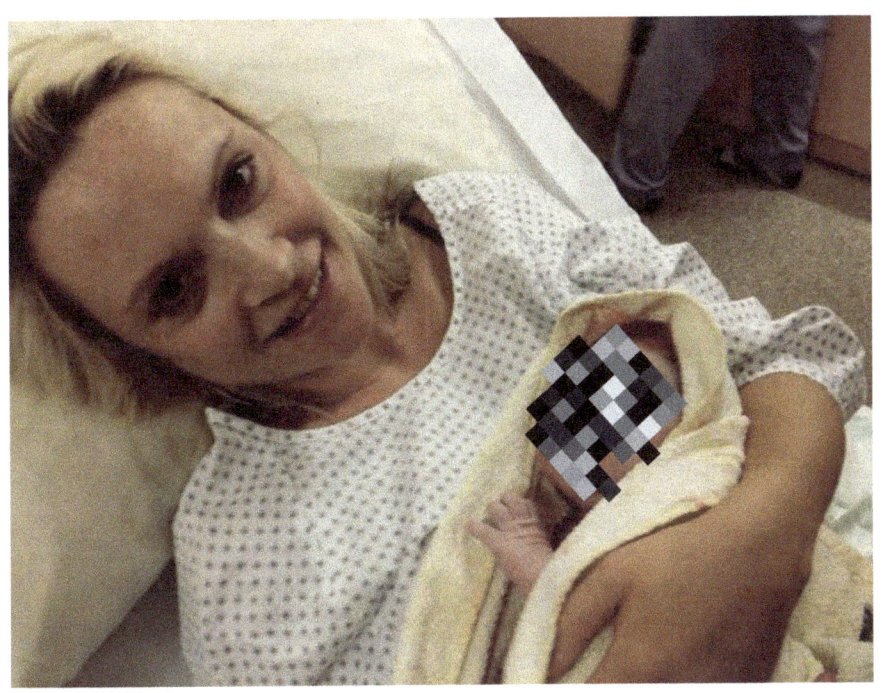

Levi Ayden was born - September 2014

On the day we had to say our final goodbyes to our friends and family, we were standing in our completely empty house, only Lui's room was still all as it was. We wanted to give him the most precious experience without any disruption during the time we were planning our departure. My parents, siblings and friends came over to say goodbye. It was a very emotional farewell, especially knowing that this one way ticket would be our final step in a new future and that our parents' grandkids would grow up not being near them. I will never forget this moment: my dad was the last person to leave the house and he gave little two-year-old Lui his model tractor that he always so adored. I had never seen my dad cry before and the memory of it still breaks my heart. I did not know what to say. I felt my heart ripping into pieces, even though I wanted to leave to build a better life for us.

The lump that I had in my throat that day did not go away for several months after. Every time I closed my eyes at night, I could see my dad crying because of the pain I made him go through by taking his grandkids away.

Stephanie came by that afternoon, and she offered to drop us at the airport. I was glad that no one in our family was going to be there, because that would have made it even harder. My husband didn't like Stephanie at all and always told me that he can't stand her. He wasn't very keen that she was dropping us at the airport, but I really wanted to have my bestie with me, saying goodbye for the last time.

At the airport, I still felt that lump in my throat, and Stephanie promised me that nothing would get in the way of our friendship. I put all my trust in her and believed that our friendship was safe. I felt so grateful to have her in my life and I knew that every challenge we would face, we would overcome together – especially the distance between Australia and Germany.

Back in Australia, we arrived to an empty apartment. We didn't take any furniture from Germany so I was excited to buy new furniture and make it our home. It was tiny, but beautiful. We were walking distance to the beach and we had a pool, sauna and gym at our apartment complex. It all felt different from three years ago, especially since we now had two children with us. But I loved the beach lifestyle, the weather and the welcoming people everywhere. And just like that, I felt like I was home again.

The boys adapted so well in Australia. Lui asked about his grandparents every day, but we assured him that we would see them very soon. I was so relieved that Lui made the transition very well, considering he was still super young. Levi was just a few weeks old, so the move didn't really affect him much.

A day after giving birth to Levi

I spent a lot of time with my husband's boss' wife again. He was working insane hours and without any family support I began to feel quite overwhelmed being on my own a lot of the time with two small kids. And still somehow, I felt guilty about that – I had everything I'd ever wanted – a wonderful husband, two darling children and a beautiful home in a country I had really come to love. I had built up so much in the six years that we lived in Sydney.

Leaving the country for three years and coming back was a brand new start. Nothing was like it was before. When we moved I had to give up my little children's fashion business in Germany; I brought most of the clothes that I still had in stock with me and I thought that I could start it up again, as soon as the container arrived.

I seemed to be constantly having to start from scratch. Picking up and leaving behind things that I had built up, including friendships wasn't easy. I've since realised every move we made was all for my husband. I gave up my career, hobbies and community to fly from one end of the world to the other, all for him. Why wouldn't I, though? He was my dream man, I loved him and we were a team.

The beach is my happy place

Back in Sydney with two little kids under the age of three, I needed to find my place again. What would it be? Would I go back to teaching and directing at the preschool? Would I just stay at home with the boys until they were old enough to go to school? Would I carry on with the children's fashion and find a new group of mums to connect with? I wasn't sure at this point, but I knew it had to be something.

My husband was instantly a wonderful father. It was clear that he adored his boys and I will be forever grateful for the intensity of his love for them. When he came home from work, he always spent time with them, and put his own needs aside for his family.

Something was missing, though. I was feeling a bit low about myself. Not having my existing mums group around me and trying to connect with other mums in the area was exhausting. I didn't like the way I looked and hated feeling frumpy, even though I still loved to dress up and wear the latest fashion; it just didn't seem to sit right on me. It was all in my mind, though. There were a few times that bulimic thoughts popped into my head but I never acted on them. After three years, I was sure I didn't want to go back down that road and I was over it for good.

Just as I didn't put on much weight during my first pregnancy with Lui, I didn't put on much with Levi either. Plus, I was quite fortunate that I lost most of the weight I did gain in the first four weeks. I was breastfeeding, so I wasn't too concerned about my calorie intake as I was burning it all right off again after feeding my baby. Levi was such an easy baby and I really enjoyed breastfeeding this time. With your second baby it all of a sudden becomes all different. I wasn't as worried or stressed, neither during the pregnancy nor with my responsibilities as a mum. It was an altogether different experience with Levi compared to my postpartum with Lui.

I spent a lot of time on social media, posting about our new life in Sydney and staying in contact with my friends. One day I stumbled across an ad on a German mums page on Facebook. It said they were looking for a native German speaker and that it was a work-from-home position. Well, that sounded exactly like me.

The only thing I felt truly confident about then was my ability to speak German, so I checked it out further. It was a beauty company, and the job was basically selling makeup and skin care through social media and the internet. I was never a salesperson, I wasn't wildly sociable and didn't really use a lot of makeup, but I needed a distraction. So I signed up.

I had to pay for my starter kit, which my husband wasn't too happy about, but I told him I needed a hobby and the worst that could happen was that I ended up with a box full of high quality makeup for a great price. He eventually got over his reservations.

The day the kit arrived was so special. My dad was visiting us from Germany, Lui had just turned three and was finally starting to sleep through the night, and Levi continued to be the easiest little baby, breastfeeding and sleeping four solid hours through the night. I had finally got into a routine, walking the boys to the next park or beach every day and slowly making friends again.

I was amazed at the products I had received in the starter kit and fell in love with them instantly. Being passionate about something helps you to sell it – something I discovered when I had my kids clothing shop in Germany. I was obsessed with baby fashion and it sold itself. I had never owned expensive makeup or skincare, so this was really special for me. The mascara was my favourite product, it gave me the longest lashes ever. Taking before and after photos became my new distraction. I wanted every woman to see how incredible this mascara was.

Experimenting with my new makeup

I used to buy overpriced designer mascara, because it was apparently good. Compared to this one, it was not even half as great. So I began connecting with people on social media and became more confident about using the products and how they could actually make a positive difference in women's lives.

Maybe that sounds a bit flippant, but I truly believe that if you feel good on the outside, it can really help you to feel good on the inside too. The same goes for fashion. Today, I love seeing the incredible transformation that happens in my personal styling client's lives after I've had a session with them. It's so empowering!

Connecting with people through social media was so much fun and I was amazed at the true connections I made with other like-minded mums again. My excitement about the whole thing must have rubbed off because I garnered a lot of interest in what I was posting. In today's world, authenticity really is a big commodity and I think in my naiveté, it was something that I put across without thinking. I was just doing me, online – showing people out there what I loved and gave them glimpses of my life, including my challenges.

Between caring for my boys and trying to connect with my husband when he was home, working with my little online side gig was really fulfilling me. That had been the missing piece in my life. When you find something you love, it really doesn't feel like work at all.

Especially connecting with like-minded women, helping them overcome their challenges with their skin and showing them how to apply makeup while being a stay-at-home mum as well.

I created group events and spoke on different topics each week, and more and more people started to follow me and watch my videos. I helped women just like me to feel more confident about themselves. I wanted to share with them that we are all in the same boat, struggling with similar things and that when we stick together and help each other, we can overcome a lot of things. I knew that there were so many beautiful mums out there longing for interaction, to have some support and guidance and to be able to feel like they were enough. I'd been through it myself. And we are enough, **more than enough**. It's just so hard to see sometimes. I knew that needed to change.

I became more and more passionate about uplifting those around me, teaching them simple makeup tricks and making their life brighter with a little makeup boost. And then... I started making money. The joy of taking myself for a simple manicure and paying for it with money I had earned was amazing. I'd forgotten what that was like. I'd always been fiercely independent and hated the times when only my husband was earning. He didn't begrudge me anything, but I always felt bad about spending money on myself instead of the family.

The thing about network marketing is that you start with friends and family, and it grows from there. I soon realised that through my excitement, I reached more people every day. I knew that putting yourself out there on social media was something special, something that could expand beyond my imagination. I built a brand without knowing what I was doing. I saw people reacting to the things I showed just because they loved the way I was presenting them. I shared not only our company's products, I shared my feelings, my daily life, my family, my dreams, my desires and my doubts. More and more people started to follow me, simply because they wanted to see what I was up to next, and I gave them what they wanted. I shared value every day, uplifted those around me and gave people compliments for simple efforts.

I felt like the world would become a better place if women supported each other. I made this my mission. I built up an elite leadership status team within my first six months. The first big promotion and the first big pay cheque blew my mind. I felt proud of myself, of my team, of what we had created, what we had achieved – all online.

I was a leader – it was an astounding thing. From being a depressed stay-at-home mum in Germany, now I was influencing people and leading a team of incredible women. I saw that I could help people and inspire them. I wanted to show all these mums out there that they could do what I did. Sit in their bathroom, put on makeup, their kids all over them and still show up; be happy and get excited about a product that makes them feel good! When people relate to you, you gain their trust and they will follow you, be inspired by you and want to do what you do. This is what I taught my team; get on their level and show people how you can transform your own life with simple things each day.

I joined a hundred online groups with native speaking Germans that lived in other countries. Even though the company hadn't yet launched in Germany, I knew that Germany would be a good market for me - I understood the culture and how to engage with them. But the German launch was six months away, so I also started building up an Australian team.

I posted some ads looking for German speakers that wanted to work their own hours. All they needed was WIFI and a phone. I was looking for mums and au pairs, immigrants, people who had moved from Germany to another country – German people that could also speak English. Many Germans are quite sceptical, but those that leave Germany to live abroad are more likely to be risk-takers; and that's what I wanted. This was not a 9-5 job. You had to work really hard to get it going. You had to leave your comfort zone and keep trying. You have to be strong willed and not give up when there is a hurdle. You can't fail in this business, unless you give up. I knew that when I built up a team with women who were strong, brave, committed and hungry to represent a mission that empowers women, we could be so successful. But I was even more inspired by the message we would get across and how powerful we can all grow when women support each other.

I got really creative with my content and I guess that's the good side of social media; the ability to reach thousands of people across the globe. I found that I really enjoyed coming up with ways to entertain my followers and they really inspired me to do more. My husband still didn't quite understand what I was up to, but he did enjoy seeing me make my own money. Even he saw how good it was for my confidence to be doing something that was successful.

He did tell me that my videos needed to be more professional, but I really disagreed – I wanted to show other women out there that I was just like them. A busy mum who just wanted to make some money on the side and look good at the same time, without sacrificing time with her children. And I know that's what made my videos and posts so popular. You don't have to be professional to be successful. You have to be authentic and passionate.

I had never been a selfie-type person so to create my first posts on social media showing off the products, it meant I took about sixty photographs to get one good one. And even then, they weren't great. But I learned. Now, I only need to take two or three to get a good one.

I began this new adventure in April and by August when the German market finally opened up, I had spent all my free time (which wasn't much) translating the product information into German so that when the products were ready to sell, we knew we could sell them in Germany. I started up a launch group for people interested in the products and the opportunity to work from home. I learned so much about the products and I worked really hard to make sure I tried out every single product and had tested each one for a while to ensure I could give my genuine and authentic feedback and advice on the products.

I recruited a number of women in Germany and trained them on how to sell the products. Of course my bestie was in it with me and extremely encouraging. By the time September came and the company was open to German orders, we already had a huge cache of pre-orders to fill. It was a great month.

That September I hit a record target and was promoted to a new level: leadership. It made me feel all the more confident. My sponsor was right there alongside me, empowering me in a way I'd never experienced before. She taught me so much about how to be there for your team and I owe a lot to her.

She always pushed me to greater achievements and saw something in me that I'd never seen. She was and still is one of my biggest inspirations. Leading with your heart and soul. She showed me how to empower those around me, by being selfless and putting yourself in the background to make others shine.

I started earning a lot more than I had previously and I got even hungrier to succeed. The team was really excited and we managed to sell and expand our team more and more. Six months later we hit the next target and promotion – I became very success driven, especially knowing that my husband and I wanted that lovely house with a pool, and to fly to Germany with the boys at least once a year.

Finally I felt I could start contributing financially to our dream. And the best part was that I loved what I was doing. I grew so much and started becoming someone that I'd never seen in myself before. Having struggled with my confidence and self-esteem all my life, I never felt like I was good enough. All because I had never learned to love myself in a way that every woman should. For the first time, I felt true happiness through empowering others and helping them build a business. Being a mum myself, I could relate to so many women out there who were feeling overwhelmed, lonely and lost. I made it my mission to empower those beauties around me to help them see their true potential; the inner and outer beauty. This uplifting movement was an incredible journey for anyone that needed a little confidence boost.

INTROSPECTION

When your work drives you to the point of intense fulfilment, you're really winning at life. And it doesn't have to even be work - it could be a hobby or just doing something that makes your heart soar. It's such a beautiful thing and I truly hope that every woman can find that in her life.

1. Imagine discovering a passion in your life that brings you immense joy and fulfilment, to the point where work feels more like pleasure than a traditional job. How does this newfound sense of purpose and enthusiasm impact your overall happiness and well-being?

2. Reflecting on your journey of finding your groove and pursuing your passion, what challenges or obstacles have you encountered along the way? How have these challenges shaped your commitment and determination to continue following your passion, even when faced with adversity?

3. As you immerse yourself in your passion and experience the thrill of doing what you love, how do you strike a balance between work and personal life? How do you ensure that

your passion remains a source of joy and doesn't become overwhelming or all-consuming?

4. In moments when doubt or uncertainty arise, how do you maintain your motivation and drive for pursuing your passion? What strategies do you employ to stay focused and inspired, even during challenging times? How does your passion help you overcome obstacles and push through setbacks?

5. As you continue to thrive in your chosen field of passion, how do you envision the future? How can you further nurture and develop your skills and expertise, and what steps can you take to continue growing and evolving within your chosen pursuit?

CHAPTER SEVEN | MOVING ON UP

"The strongest actions for a woman is to love herself, be herself and shine amongst those who never believed she could."
— Unknown

That year, two weeks before Christmas, my husband was made redundant. It was a big blow for him, but he was incredibly experienced and brilliant at what he did, so it didn't take long for him to find another job. Unfortunately, that job was in Brisbane. I didn't want to leave Sydney. I had just started to find my feet again and build up a life here.

Brisbane and Sydney are so different, they could be two different countries. Sydney is very cosmopolitan and we'd lived on the Northern Beaches, whereas Queensland always seemed so much more casual and relaxed. I love new challenges and I'm actually quite good with change. Saying goodbye and starting again was pretty much one of our main things in the past couple of years. So, even though I didn't want to go, I knew it would be a new opportunity to expand my connections. I was getting good at starting over from scratch in a different country.

His new job meant that he would be travelling a lot and we needed to find a home near the airport. We found a house to rent near the water but the beach culture wasn't the same as it was in Sydney. Coming from the most prestigious area in Sydney, where people live the beach lifestyle - surfing, mesmerising sunsets, brunch with ocean views and very successful people everywhere, Brisbane seemed very different. Today, after living in Brisbane for over eight years, I love every bit of it. It's where I call home.

It was also going to be hard on his relationship with the boys. They shared an incredibly special bond and he always made all of us laugh. I felt lonely without him and I never liked it when he was travelling. It was really tough on all of us.

Once again, we had to say goodbye to our friends in Sydney and I missed them terribly. My husband never really had good friends. He got along with his work colleagues and had that one work mate that he could bitch about everything with. He was just not that guy who was interested in getting to know people and growing friendships. I was the complete opposite. I loved to meet new people and get to know their personalities. I never judged anyone and I connected with so many people that he thought were 'not in our league' – whatever that meant.

If I like someone I don't care where they come from, I don't care what they look like, or if they have a university degree. He never really liked my friends, they were always too loud, too much, too poor, too uneducated or simply didn't like him.

I threw myself into building my business. I was already doing really well, and my teams were motivated to keep going on the same trajectory. It's amazing how success breeds success. The more you feel it, the more you want it. I set up a little studio in our living room and made videos every day. I was getting better at them too.

Sometimes I look back and try to remember where it started to really explode in my down line, I try to remember the shift. But there was never a specific moment, or an explosion of sudden success. It was gradually happening every single day, moving closer to my goals. Did I have a plan? Did I map this all out? Was I experienced enough to know what I was doing at the time? Absolutely not! And that's my biggest piece of advice to anyone in business. Just do it. Trust your passion, be excited, show up every day, identify the people who have an influence, work with the runners, always make sure that you are putting at least 80% of your time into your own business, like your own sales, your own recruiting and building your network every single day.

I joined mum's groups and local community Facebook pages to connect to people who I could hang out with, with whom I could share my passion for my business, and of course, to make friends. I eventually started connecting with local mums, meeting up for playdates with the boys. I talked to everyone around me about the incredible work we were doing with the company. I loved everything we stood for; empowering women and creating a sisterhood like I had never experienced before.

I always loved helping women and bringing like-minded women together. Considering all the uplifting things I had done before – the mum's group in Germany, teaching German, building up the preschool in Sydney – this was the greatest experience by far with the greatest impact. I felt extremely passionate about not only the products, but the vision as well. I learnt an incredible amount about how to apply makeup correctly and how to enhance your natural features. I wanted to scream this out to the world and let everyone know how confident you can become when you believe in yourself.

I travelled to America for a leadership event and this trip brought me even closer to my vision and my dreams. I documented every single thing and shared it with my team. I hoped they would be inspired by it. I couldn't wait to cheer them on, once they achieved an incredible trip like this. Leadership became a whole new passion for me.

After a few months we decided that we really needed to buy a home – it seemed that Brisbane was where we would end up staying and it was a good idea to put down some proper roots. But it wasn't an easy task. He and I both wanted specific things in a house. I dreamed of a walk-in closet and a double story, while he wanted a double garage and huge yard. Within the budget we had set, there wasn't anything that met our requirements.

After viewing what felt like hundreds of unsuitable homes, we decided we'd have to adjust our budget – and then we finally found the home we wanted. In a new estate that was further away from the city and the airport, but the house was incredibly modern, with all the finishes we wanted.

It was a display home, the only one in the area, so of course it came with many exclusive extras, like a wooden staircase with glass railing. The garden was fully established with palm trees and plants. It had a huge double garage and lots of space and storage. The backyard was big and we could already envision the pool being established one day. It even had enough space to build a shed, something he'd always wanted. The master bedroom was beautiful, it had only a small walk-in wardrobe which I could accept since everything else was perfect. I imagined our furniture in it and pictured us walking around as a family, living our dream life.

The house was on a double block of land, so the neighbours weren't too close and it was right next to a wetland with a beautiful view. It was open, with high ceilings and loads of light. I remember walking in and saying to him, "I love this, I want it." He hissed at me to shut up and not say anything stupid in front of the agent. He wanted to play that game where you look only a little bit interested so he could start negotiating the price down. We did get it at a lower price because it was a bit expensive for the area.

We were really happy in the end. I've never felt so excited. For the first time I felt at home in Brisbane, as we would have never been able to afford a house like that in Sydney. It took us about eight weeks to fully settle in and make it our dream home.

My husband loved working in the garden and being with the boys in the big yard, playing and teaching them all sorts of things. I adored looking out to see them together, chattering away, big smiles on all their faces.

My business continued to grow and I started to host some in-home parties. I had never wanted to host them and had hated being invited to those sales parties in the past. But there I was, rocking up with my makeup trunk full of goodies and a big smile on my face, ready to empower some beautiful women.

I ended up loving every second of it and people always told me afterwards that they could see my passion for the industry, especially helping women to become confident and raise their self-esteem. Sometimes there is a pressure that comes with looking a certain way and I feel like I've fallen into this category. Even though I am what the world deems 'pretty', it's crystal clear that your looks don't always determine your confidence and self-esteem. I'm a walking example of that. We all walk through life with our own issues and it's so important to look past a person's appearance to see the real human inside. Just because I look a certain way doesn't mean that I am always confident, always happy, or have an easy life.

I ordered some hard copy catalogues to hand out to my customers and I proudly told my group that they never used professional models. Instead, those pretty faces were all ambassadors within our company. I wondered what it would be like to be one of them. Being on the cover as a model, representing the company and the products would make me so proud.

Each year ten women from the company of over one million women were chosen to be in the catalogue. It was a huge privilege and certainly helped your business to be featured. It was part of their marketing, using their salesforce as the models and it really wasn't about being beautiful or super slim – it was about how you represented the company and how you lived their mission: to uplift, empower and validate. How you presented the products, how you lived your life and how you got involved in helping others played a big part in being considered for the catalogue.

Women were nominated to be in the catalogue, by top-level leaders or the VP of Marketing. I dreamed of being in the catalogue because of how it would inspire other women to follow their dreams and not give up on anything that seems unreachable but yet so incredible. I could show all these wonderful humans what is possible if only you have the audacity to dream it. Every night when I went to bed, I closed my eyes and visualised my face on the cover of that catalogue. All I could dream of was seeing my face being displayed on a big billboard; people driving past and thinking, "I didn't give up, and I grew into my strongest self because of her." So I kept dreaming and I knew one day that would become my reality.

For me that represented discipline, dedication, success, integrity, commitment, inspiration, empowerment, hard work, inner beauty and NEVER quitting. All the things I wanted to be associated with. I really didn't think that I would ever be nominated, but it was a dream for everyone who was in the business. We all looked up to the catalogue models, because it was the highest validation and recognition you could get. And I just kept manifesting it every night in my dreams.

The co-owner always made the final decision about which nominees would appear in the catalogue. She took this very seriously and looking after the models was one of her favourite tasks. The models were flown in from across the world and got to spend time with her during the shoot.

One cold, Queensland winter morning I remember driving in the car with my husband and the boys, when I got a friend request from her on Facebook. I was stunned that the owner would want to connect with me and, of course, I immediately accepted the request. My husband couldn't understand why I thought it was such a big deal, even though he knew I was putting my all into the company. I adored this woman and everything she had accomplished, how invested she was to help other people and see true beauty in everyone around her. She assessed all the nominees to see how closely they were living the mission and values of the company. This meant I had been nominated and I was over the moon.

Although I was ecstatic to simply be nominated, the next three days were a rollercoaster of emotions for me. One moment I was over the moon at just being nominated, and the next I was full of fear that I wouldn't get chosen. I spent a lot of time exercising to keep myself calm. I felt like I was in a bubble that could burst at any moment. I saw all these beautiful women posting about getting friend requests from the co-owner and I began to doubt my chances. I really wanted it at this point, there was no way back. I checked my inbox incessantly, longing for that message from her... but nothing. The waiting and the not knowing was the worst.

On the morning of that third day, I woke up to see a message from her in my inbox and I nearly fell out of bed. I'D BEEN CHOSEN!

Her words to me are still stuck in my head – she said I was a true beauty and she loved the way I was presenting the products and sharing my family life over here in Australia. I dropped my phone and screamed. My husband rushed upstairs to ask what was wrong and found me on the bathroom floor shaking and crying happy tears.

I was on cloud nine! Throughout my life, I hadn't ever felt like I was quite good enough for anything. And now I'd been chosen from a pool of so many incredible women to be in the catalogue for a company that had truly changed my life. Nobody, not even my grumpy husband, could burst my happy bubble. He wasn't enthusiastic at all – in fact, he was quite dismissive about the whole thing. I think he still saw my business as a hobby. My mind started to race: Who would look after the boys while I was away? How long would I be gone for?

The catalogue photoshoot was a week-long affair in the United States, and I was to fly there in November. It was all the motivation I needed to push even harder and make more sales. In October that year, I leapt up to the next level in the business – the second time in six months. I wanted to fly over to the US as a success and I was so proud of myself for doing it.

I've never been more motivated to reach a new promotion than I was that month. I had been chosen for the catalogue and my team was absolutely hysterical. I wanted to be a role model, show them how you can pursue your dreams and that you should never give up on your goals. NEVER.

I was excited to take my team on a journey of empowering success, showing them what can be achieved by simply believing you are a success.

Since I was coming from Australia, further than anyone else, I was flown out a few days before the other women. From the minute I landed I was treated like royalty – I stayed in a gorgeous hotel and was treated with loads of pampering and gifts every day. When the others arrived, we all began our days at 7am with makeup and styling and then spent most of the day being photographed.

Each night, a different member of the company's management took us out to dinner. It was amazing because we got to learn about every aspect of the business – from product development to IT. I devoured all the information – I was so enjoying being part of something that was really making a fundamental difference to the lives of so many women. And I'm not just talking about the incredible products, I'm talking about the upliftment, the validation, the empowerment. All the things I searched and longed for each time we relocated.

I felt like a supermodel after that trip. The only downside was my husband's attitude. He would phone me all the time and tell me the boys were crying for me, and that I should be home with them. It was the first time I'd ever been away from my boys, so I felt guilty enough as it was. His constant calling and moaning really put a damper on the trip for me. If I didn't answer the phone or didn't message him back right away, he got angry. It wasn't something I was used to – perhaps he was feeling guilty? I tried to explain to him one night that it was really hard for me to message and call, because of the time difference and the tight schedule we had. He didn't understand it at all. In fact, he doubted my priorities as a mother. I wished he could be more like the other women's husbands, who were so supportive and just wanted them to enjoy every moment of the experience.

The catalogue came out the next March. My sponsor and dear friend said to me, you'll not only be on the cover, you will be at the top of the company. She saw it happening and nothing motivated me more than that.

And we did it! The motivation was so high. No one had been promoted within our company in Australia for years and I wanted to hit the top with my team, because I believed we had the ability, the strength and the commitment to do just that. I wanted this so badly for my team. I knew every leadership promotion would change their lives as much as it changed mine. I felt proud; proud of sticking to my values, my dedication, the love and effort I'd put into building connections and relationships. The amount of time I'd spent with women to empower them and help them find their confidence, make them feel good about themselves and help them to build a strong solid business.

The best part of the business though, was being able to include my boys. Working from home afforded me the opportunity to spend time with them, drop them off and pick them up from school and attend all their school events. It meant the world not only to them, but to me as well. It's the best feeling ever! I could be a full-time business owner, and an involved and hands-on mum. Plus, my boys enjoyed experimenting with makeup alongside me and they loved being in front of the camera too. They became little heroes within my team since they always got involved in my daily lives and tutorials. My network wanted to see that too – it made me more relatable as a busy, working mum striving for success while being present with her children.

One morning about a month after my trip to the US, I woke up to at least five hundred messages and thousands of tags from women all over the world on my socials. I opened my Facebook to see a video of the Headquarters in America getting plastered with a huge image of me and the word UPLIFT underneath. Once again, I nearly fell out of bed. I just couldn't believe my eyes. They were actually putting my face on their five-story, 160,000 square foot building!

One of the greatest moments in my life, seeing my face on the headquarter building in Utah

INTROSPECTION

When a dream comes true, there's nothing quite like the feeling. But when the person you most want to support you and be proud of you doesn't seem to care, it can be devastating.

1. Imagine having a burning desire to obtain something that you truly, deeply want. How does this intense longing and aspiration serve as a driving force in your life, pushing you to work harder and overcome obstacles in pursuit of your goal?

2. Reflecting on your journey to attain what you truly desire, what challenges or setbacks have you encountered along the way? How have these obstacles fuelled your determination and strengthened your resolve to achieve your goal? How does the pursuit of your deepest desires shape your character and personal growth?

3. In the face of adversity, how do you maintain unwavering motivation and perseverance to obtain what you truly want? What strategies do you employ to stay focused, resilient, and

committed to your goal, even when faced with discouragement or setbacks?

4. Now, imagine having a life partner who does not support you and makes you feel bad for your success. How does their lack of support impact your pursuit of your desires? How do you navigate the tension between seeking what you want and managing the negativity or unsupportive behaviour from your partner?

5. Reflecting on the experience of having a life partner who doesn't support your success, how does it affect your self-esteem and overall well-being? How do you manage the emotional toll it takes on you and find ways to stay motivated and confident despite their lack of support? How can you cultivate a support system outside of your partner to help fuel your ambition and belief in yourself?

CHAPTER EIGHT | TAKING OFF

"There are two different types of people in the world, those who want to know, and those who want to believe."
— Friedrich Nietzsche

As predicted, things really took off from there. Since I had pushed my team so hard, and because they were so motivated within themselves, we were doing better than ever. The business' system worked on different levels and as a leader, I was given a cash bonus whenever my team achieved specific goals. We were hitting all the goals and regularly moved to the next level of success. When I moved up, then so did other members of my team – so we all won.

My passion for seeing women succeed, making them stronger and showing them how to use their abilities to create an uplifting, empowering sisterhood grew stronger with every success we achieved together.

That year both my husband and I travelled a lot. I was invited to speak at several international conferences and big events as a keynote speaker and I flew to every event that would take me further in my career. I learned so much about building a huge business and leading from the heart. I started to duplicate my actions and my team got stronger every month.

Speaking as an international keynote in Frankfurt, Germany

With all our respective travelling, my husband and I got into a routine of taking turns, managing to schedule trips so that one of us was always home with the kids. It was great to come back home after a few days of being away and spend time with the kids again. I appreciated us as a family even more because we were able to do this. Our boys grew up bilingual of course, I always wanted them to speak two languages fluently as this would open so many more doors for them. We spoke German with them from birth, the English part came automatically once they started to go to kindergarten in Australia.

With me running my own business and being flexible with hours I could offer my boys so much more time and possibilities than other working mums. I always felt very proud and fortunate to do this. It was a dream come true. Following my passion to empower women and getting paid for it, while also not missing out on having my babies with me all the time.

The boys got used to seeing me doing live videos, being on Zoom calls, getting up in the middle of the night for personal development workshops and presenting the products each day. Including them in everything I did not only made me more relatable to my network, but also showed my boys the value of hard work and the importance of a strong work ethic. It was vital for me to be present for the kids while achieving success in my business, even if it was difficult and meant I never got a quiet moment to myself. I don't believe that my husband ever saw how much or how hard I was working at the time. Being a full-time mum while being a full-time business owner and leader takes a lot of effort; an effort I think he took for granted all those years.

I loved being a leader and changing lives. I realised quite quickly that *being* a good leader is one thing and *building* good leaders is another. I believe one hundred percent that when you uplift those around you with respect, love, excitement and honesty you will duplicate your down line and create more leaders. I never looked at numbers or how much people were selling, I validated the ones who created amazing things, who showed up, did the work, and helped others. An empowered person will do incredible things.

If you want to grow into a great leader, you cannot be afraid of people being better than you or take pride in the accomplishments of those that you help along the way. Help others reach their goals, always be honest and courageous, lead with intention, humility and integrity. Be trustworthy and recognize accomplishments, be empathetic and have a clear focus. Trust in people's expertise and exemplify the culture. Build self-efficacy through sufficient resources and hold your team members accountable. Share your passion and let others lead the same way. Uplift, empower, and validate them and make this your leadership mission.

Speaking in London at the European convention

My best friend, Stephanie, was right there with me every step of the way. Over and above the work we did together, we also spoke every day on a personal level. She knew everything about me and my life and I knew seemingly everything about hers – she was my rock, that person I could both cry and laugh with. She always had the best advice and she was always there for me. We shared every tiny detail of our lives. Of course, that meant we spoke about our relationships too – so she knew when one of the boys did something clever or naughty and she knew how I felt about my husband every single day. She complained about her husband a lot and I could feel she wasn't really happy, but she always pulled through.

2019 was the best year I'd ever had in the business. I had a lot of women within my organisation, my front-line leaders were killing it, and I absolutely loved the process of building them up, making them even stronger and helping them to form a solid team within their business. I was working non-stop, often in the middle of the night, doing Zoom calls, attending corporate meetings and doing personal development.

Telling my story on stage at an international event in Germany

I was living my best life! I just loved what I was doing. Feeding into other people's lives and getting such brilliant feedback made me incredibly confident and I was really happy. I was finally happy with my body; the business changed my mindset and strengthened my self-esteem to make me the strongest version of myself that I'd ever been. Every day I felt that I was growing into the woman I had always wanted to become. I had overcome bulimia and no longer had the urge to purge after I had eaten a meal that I really enjoyed. I felt happy, strong and complete. That's what I wanted to bring out in women all over the globe.

I was invited to a number of international events to speak, as well as company conferences and incentive trips. That meant I was travelling quite a bit. My dream life had become a reality. Being a leader and running a not-so-little beauty business became one of my favourite parts. I did many leadership courses, signed up for workshops, read all the books about being a great leader and growing in your organisation. I learnt the importance of being on the same level as those you are leading. I always saw my team perform their best and felt their motivation through the community the most when I was transparent, vulnerable, and shared my emotions and struggles. The connection with my team got stronger every time. People only connect with you when they can relate. We all have our struggles, no one is perfect, no one gets successful without a struggle, no one has an easy ride to the top. I showed them how I struggled, but also how I overcame my struggles. I shared my feelings and built trust.

Speaking about leadership and mindset

Being recognised for reaching the top of the company

My own sales were really great and I had an excellent client base. I was going live on social media daily, with loads of people watching my tutorials. They felt inspired and I was certainly inspired by that in return.

Another dream came true; we were finally able to build our pool in the yard. I also paid for my dad to come over to visit us, which for me was the best feeling. I bought my dream car and we spoiled the boys every weekend; theme parks, going out for dinner and new bikes.

But, the more confident I became, the more distant my husband seemed. He was still job hopping, looking for the next best thing. During that year I was earning more than him – which, as with many men, didn't really sit that well with him. He never really admitted it, because he loved seeing my paycheque at the end of each month, but I began to notice a pattern of his discontent. He was simply never quite satisfied with whatever was going on in his life, especially his work. He consistently thought he knew better than anyone else and I don't think he expected me to make such a success out of my 'hobby'. He probably didn't get much recognition at work and I remember that there was always some sort of drama. He often seemed very stressed, not satisfied or happy with what he was doing.

He didn't like any of my friends and didn't have many of his own. As a result, I was the only one with which he could let out his anger and frustration. It was fine with me. I did the same with him, if there was anything that I got upset about. For me, friends mean the world and I was so glad to have incredible people around me, and I never felt like I missed out on having good conversations. I'd always wanted a life where we had a group of good friends to go on double dates with and enjoy each other's company. But he just didn't manage to get on with my friends' partners – he always found something not to like. I really wished for a circle of like-minded friends that we could hang out with, and include our children.

If we went out with other couples it was often a very uncomfortable situation, as he always found something that I had said or done to point out in an embarrassing moment. He laughed about how I pronounced certain words and made me feel small. Me being quite confident, I pretended to find it funny, even though I hated those situations. As long as he could make fun of someone, he was in a happy mood. It makes me think back to how he used to tease my brother years before back in Germany.

I made many connections in my business and it felt like a beautiful sisterhood. It would have been so natural to include their families in that scenario. I remember going to speak at a conference in Germany and by then, everyone knew me because of the catalogue and the amount of work I did; not only on my team, other teams as well. I poured all my energy, my heart and soul into this beautiful mission. Our team was called the Team of Hearts because we had no drama, no negativity, and no gossip within our ranks. I strongly encouraged a positive mindset within our community and by now I had read so many books about leadership, that I developed my own perspective on how to lead an empire with your heart and through building strong relationships.

My husband never came to any of my events, simply because he wasn't really interested, and of course, he looked after the boys when I was travelling and vice versa. In 2019, I travelled to five international countries and he was away for work quite a bit too. The boys really got used to it and we found that it was great for them to experience and observe how we were working hard for them and us as a family.

That year, we all took a trip to Germany. I attended a conference with thousands of people and my husband joined me for the first time. Naturally, Stephanie was also there to support me, sitting in the row behind us. She was quite hyper, giggling all the time and acting a bit over-the-top, which was strange, but I thought maybe she was just excited for me. Of course, I didn't expect my husband to be present the whole time. I hadn't noticed that Stephanie had spent a lot of time outside during this conference until some friends mentioned it to me later – they had seen Stephanie and my husband chatting outside. I thought it was strange since he never really liked her, but maybe it was a good thing that he was getting to know my best friend.

I was the international keynote speaker. There was big pressure for me to really pull it off. Speaking on stage was something I loved, and it became a space where I could inspire others and help them grow further in their business through my knowledge. I think it was the first time he realised just how successful I had become. While he saw me working all hours of the day and night and knew that I was making good money, he wasn't prepared for the onslaught of 'fans' I had garnered. Women were lining up to hug and greet me, give me presents, take photos with me and some even wanted an autograph. Thousands of women knew my name, followed my journey and felt inspired by my leadership and success.

I spent all day connecting with those women, as I really wanted them to feel uplifted and valued. I made the effort to talk to every single one of them. I felt so honoured and proud to be their role model and I wanted every single woman to feel the same. I see great potential in everyone. Most of these girls wanted to be in a leadership position and I was here to help them reach that goal. If you want to grow into a great leader, you can't be afraid of people being better than you or take pride in the accomplishments of those that you help along the way. Help others to reach their goals, always be honest and courageous, lead with intention, humility and integrity. Be trustworthy and recognize accomplishments, be empathetic and have a clear focus. Trust in people's expertise and exemplify the culture. Build self-efficacy through sufficient resources and hold your team members accountable. Share your passion and let others lead the same way. Uplift, empower and validate them – make this your leadership mission.

My husband and I made a very handsome couple and a number of the women there wanted to get a photo with him too – but only because he was my husband. Of course, they thought he was incredibly supportive and wanted to meet the man that was with me. I could see that he thought they were just interested in him and thankfully that fluffed up his ego a bit.

But our relationship had already taken quite a dip – with the long hours I was working, especially at night since I had a team and customers all over the world. We were a little like ships passing in the night. We certainly weren't intimate for quite a while. I didn't think it was a big deal because I was so wrapped up in my work, and he never expressed that he needed or wanted me in that way at all. I should have seen it though.

However, looking back it was strange. I didn't seem to get anything from him – no hugs, or any kind of affection. I kind of gave up on it. I was getting all the validation and words of encouragement I needed from the business. I had come to realise that I am enough the way I am; I was finally confident in my own skin. I was no longer craving attention from him. I no longer needed him to validate me as the woman I've always wanted to be. I was her now.

We were still doing family things together and would spend every weekend with the kids. We probably looked like the ideal family. But was that my reality?

He rarely made an effort to take me out on a date night, but I didn't miss it either. He often forgot my birthday and then just asked me the day before what I would like. I think I can count on one hand the number of times he actually surprised me with something. No cards, no flowers. We joked about it and it was not really important to me, since he knew how I felt about my birthday. I knew that he loved me. I didn't know any other way.

All this time, I was getting closer and closer to Stephanie. She was one of my true stars in the business and I felt like she would always be there for me. We trained the team and new recruits together and whenever we went away to a conference, we would share a room. We sent voice messages every day, spoke on the phone or made video calls. She was my rock, my safe place, my partner in crime, my girl, my best friend. She was the only person in my life who truly understood me. She worked so hard every day, and she really did embody the ethos of the company.

We'd bonded beautifully when we reconnected back in Germany, but this was on a different level. We really did share everything – she knew when I was travelling, when my husband was travelling, what I had for breakfast, what I was feeling on a daily basis, and I knew those things about her too.

My husband was becoming more and more frustrated with pretty much everything I said or did. I could not do anything right in his eyes. The way I stacked the dishwasher, how I did the laundry, the way I parked the car in the garage, how I folded the towels. Looking back, I really should have seen all those signs – I always tried my best, but it was never enough and it often came to a point where I started to experience anxiety when I heard him coming home from work. I remember the second I heard the garage door open, I would run through the whole house to make sure I folded the towels right and put them in a certain way over the rail. I quickly checked if I had forgotten to turn off any lights, or if a window was accidentally still open while the aircon was running. The first thing he did when he came home was to check all those things before he actually said hello to me. Most of the time I failed and forgot something or didn't do something to his standard. I couldn't win. I was walking on eggshells! EVERY SINGLE DAY.

It was a really good year in terms of income. He bought a motorbike and he built his shed, like he'd always wanted. What made him happy, made me happy. We went on loads of holidays with the kids and even hired an au pair from Germany – which was amazing because she was wonderful with the boys and it lessened my guilt about leaving them when I had to travel.

I distinctly remember going to the Opera one night – my husband had never really been into that kind of stuff, but we both wanted to go. I bought a beautiful dress and we enjoyed a really luxurious night of dinner and the Opera. Although I felt great in the dress, I do remember looking in the mirror and wondering what it would be like if I could fill the dress out a little more. I'd never really developed boobs, and I looked a bit like a twelve-year-old girl from the front, stuck in the body of a forty-year-old. As a teenager I had been bullied quite a bit by the boys in my classroom for not having boobs like the other girls. When I met my first boyfriend, I didn't care about it too much anymore and for my husband it had never been an issue either. I'd never thought that plastic surgery was something I'd want to have, I was actually always kind of freaked out by it, but that night, it did cross my mind.

A friend of mine had recently had hers done and she was so happy with the result. And these days, it's not a major operation – you can do them in school hours, and the recovery time isn't too arduous. All these thoughts were going through my mind during the Opera! By the time we got home, I'd made up my mind. I could afford it and I thought, "why not?" Just a little outside enhancement.

Of course, I spoke to Stephanie about it the next day and she was surprised I had even considered it. I told her that my husband was very excited as well. Her response was that my husband's opinion shouldn't be the reason that I get it done. I assured her that he had nothing to do with it, but she somehow didn't think it was a good idea. It was somewhat strange for her to not be supportive of something I wanted to do, but I didn't dwell on her lack of support. I spent quite a bit of time researching the right surgeon and finding out all there was to know. I was suddenly really excited about the whole idea. I didn't realise, though, that it was the beginning of something that would change my life completely.

INTROSPECTION

Life isn't linear – you can be happy and sad at the same time. You can feel successful and like a failure. It's the nature of life.

1. When you feel like you are at the peak of your game and everything seems to be going well, how do you navigate the tendency to overlook red flags or minor concerns in your life? How can you ensure that you maintain a balanced perspective and address any underlying issues or potential pitfalls, even during moments of great success?

2. What are some instances where you might have ignored red flags or niggling doubts? How did this oversight impact your overall well-being and decision-making? What lessons have you learned from those experiences, and how can you apply them to maintain a vigilant and discerning mindset moving forward?

3. Have you ever experienced a strong compulsion to do something that may seem frivolous or out of character for you, even when everything else in your life is seemingly on track? How did you navigate this internal drive and what was the outcome? How can these moments of indulgence or personal exploration contribute to your overall happiness and self-fulfilment?

4. In the pursuit of personal happiness and fulfilment, how can you strike a balance between following your passions and maintaining responsibilities and obligations? How do you reconcile the desire to pursue something solely for yourself, even if it may appear frivolous to others, with the need to maintain a sense of stability and harmony in your life? How can you find a middle ground that allows you to honour both your own desires and your commitments to others?

CHAPTER NINE | CRASH AND BURN

"Success is not something to wait for, it is something to work for."
— Henry Wadsworth Longfellow

Each year the company arranged incentive trips. We had to perform to a specific criterion throughout the year to receive the reward, and I was hitting those targets every time. In 2019, we were flying high, and January 2020 it was time for my incentive trip! Since my husband and I would tag-team with the boys, it made sense that he never came with me on these trips. Even so, I don't think he had any interest in joining me anyway. It also gave me the opportunity to spend quality time with my team. Nevertheless, I always felt sad seeing all the other leaders with their husbands on the trips.

Living my dream on the incentive trip - January 2020

I was invited to take a plus one for free, so I took a German friend of mine who lived in Sydney and we met up for a fun pre-trip girls' night before heading out with the others. Stephanie was there too, of course and we all had dinner together.

I was on this strict diet at the time with no alcohol, super clean eating and exercising every day. Stephanie was quite disparaging about it and told me that I was no fun when my friend and I left the dinner party early that night. Since it was quite out of character for Stephanie to be unsupportive of me, I took it as a joke even though there was a slight edge to her teasing. I didn't quite know where it was coming from. I really wished she would understand that this was very important to me. She knew that I was always extremely committed when I said yes to something.

2019 was one of the best years I've ever had in my career and quite a few girls from my team also earned the trip. I was so excited to spend some quality time with them, connect in person, and make some amazing memories together. I wanted to spend as much time as possible with my team during the trip. I bought them all presents and they surprised me with customised t-shirts with our team's name. One evening, I invited my team to my room so that we could really celebrate their success. I felt so fortunate to spend this time with them and I knew this trip would bring us all even closer.

Stephanie was acting very strangely and I couldn't understand why. Had something happened that she hadn't told me about? It was weird since we shared everything with each other. I hardly saw her the whole trip. I was hanging out with my team and she was off partying with just about anyone other than me. I simply had no idea what was wrong or if I had done something to anger her. We had spoken every single day and before the trip; we'd been talking about all the things we wanted to do, what we were going to wear, where we'd go on the day's excursions. We intended on spending the whole trip together.

One evening, Stephanie had gone out and had an absolute ball in one of the smaller bars that had a karaoke night. The next day she insisted we all do it with her again. I can't really sing but I wanted to spend time with her, so I agreed. But we didn't go to the same place she'd been the night before – this was a big production in a theatre that held a few thousand people. It was the big karaoke night and most of the people that got up on stage could actually perform. They all sounded like professionals to me. Seeing this, I backed out of singing – I was prepared to make a fool of myself in front of a bunch of other amateurs, but this was a whole different level.

Stephanie went off at me in such an awful way, telling me I wasn't a leader if I couldn't even be brave enough to go up on stage to sing. I tried to ignore her attitude. My entire team was there, along with a number of other women from the greater company. It was so humiliating! I kept telling her to stop and to let it go, but she kept going on. I tried to keep my calm and pretended it wasn't bothering me, but the situation became completely out of control and everyone around us could see and feel the tension. I tried to hold back my tears. I was disappointed in her and just couldn't understand why she would act that way.

Everyone was feeling extremely uncomfortable. My guest and I went back to our room and I found myself trying to protect Stephanie and explain her behaviour, even though I had no idea what had gotten into her. I told my friend that she was probably just overwhelmed from all the partying and even that she deserved to let her hair down a bit, considering how hard she had worked the previous year.

A few nights later I asked her if we could have dinner together because I'd hardly seen her. She agreed and suggested one of the more casual dining places, saying she didn't feel like getting all dressed up. We arrived to meet her, casually dressed but she arrived dressed-to-kill and said she'd decided to go to one of the other restaurants with some of her new friends instead. I was confused. I was disappointed. I felt let down, blindsided even. Did she plan this? Did I do something wrong to upset her? I couldn't think of anything.

A few people asked me what was going on with her and I continued to protect her, making one excuse after the next. I had no idea what to do. While we spoke every single day, we only got to see each other physically about once a year, on a trip or when I was in Germany, so her attitude towards me was incomprehensible.

The only possible explanation I could come up with at the time was that she might be a little envious of my upcoming breast augmentation. I remembered how unsupportive she was of the idea when I first told her I was considering the surgery. She had amazing breasts and perhaps that was one thing she felt that she had and I didn't. But that was a tenuous guess. I held onto it though.

When we arrived back home after the trip, it was like nothing had happened. We continued on as before, chatting and messaging daily. I considered asking her about it and talking through it, but I'm not big on conflict so I just let it slide. I was sure she had her reasons and maybe there was something that triggered her. If it had been important, I'm sure she would have come out with it. But she never did. I just filed the whole scenario under 'overthinking' in my mind. Little did I know that one day it would all make sense.

The entire world will remember 2020 for all time – the year that COVID-19 took over our lives and livelihoods. After our trip, almost everyone was ill. Thankfully, I wasn't. We had no idea at the time that it could be this dreaded virus. We'd obviously heard about it on the news, but had no reason yet to know what a massive impact it would have on our lives.

I felt like I was in the best physical condition of my life – I'd been training hard and even did my morning run each day on the trip at 6am. I was feeling good. Life was good. Even though I was nervous about my surgery, I was still looking forward to it and I was certainly ready.

Since I was over forty, I had to go for a mammogram before surgery, and I'd told the clinic I'd do it when I got back from overseas. A few days after the scan, I got a call saying that they couldn't do the operation and my heart sank. The first thought that came into my mind was, 'OMG I have breast cancer'. But they assured me that the scan was all clear; it was because there was a 21-day cooling off period because I'd been out of the country. I was relieved that I was healthy but devastated because I didn't understand the impact of COVID back then. I thought it was unnecessary, but they wouldn't let me get my surgery done.

Our au pair got the last flight out of Australia back to Germany, and it was only when we were booking her flights that I truly realised I wasn't going anywhere for a while. Then we were all locked down. Schools closed, all my flights were cancelled, many were non-refundable, and we were pretty much stuck. A whole new way of life came to the surface. Not being able to leave the house anymore and just patiently waiting for this virus to go away. We were glued to the TV for the latest news and updates on a daily basis.

We managed to find a new au pair who was able to stay with us and do homeschooling with the boys – an absolute saviour. To say that both of us working from home was difficult is a massive understatement. I know many people around the world have experienced the same. As with many things, when a good relationship is faced with a crisis, it gets stronger. However, one that already has cracks seems to crack even further. We didn't know at the time that this would be a big learning curve for us. We were about to face a monumental struggle. We knew nothing about it and we just tried our best like everyone else on this planet to make it work.

To date, 2019 was my busiest and most fortuitous year, and I know that my husband and I didn't spend much time alone together – time we needed in order to keep our relationship strong. We passed by each other, only coming together to do things as a family. I was driven and focussed on building my business and he was working long hours. It's not a new story – but it really should be a warning sign for all couples. Date nights aren't just for couples that are still dating or newly wed; they are a serious requirement for keeping a relationship on track.

Things got tough very quickly, both professionally and personally. Suddenly it was hard to get business all over the world, so many of my team were battling to keep their sales up. And of course, who really cared about a beauty routine during the pandemic? You couldn't go out and when you did, you had to cover your face anyway. While it may have been revolutionary for many in terms of going all natural, for those in our business, it spelled out disaster. I lost a number of my team leaders and that meant our sales simply didn't reach the necessary levels. The pandemic really took a big toll on everything. After all my numerous trips had been cancelled and I was not able to leave the country, nor the state, I had no idea how to survive being completely isolated.

My husband started to work from home and he took over my office space in the house. The schools were closed and the boys had to be homeschooled. Luckily, our new au pair lived with us, she spoke fluent German and was incredible with Lui and Levi. They loved her and so did I.

My husband was in Zoom meetings non-stop, all day, five days a week. I had to keep the boys quiet and calm, which was nearly impossible. We weren't supposed to leave the house at all for months. He couldn't cope with his workload and the fact that he didn't have any peace in the house, caused us to have frequent arguments, shouting at each other. The fact that I had a full-time job as well and needed space to work didn't seem to phase him.

Most of my customers didn't want to re-order until they knew when the pandemic was ending. In the space of just one month, the world was a completely different place. My team started to get frustrated in the same way. People struggled financially and of course no one was putting makeup or skincare on their priority list. A lot of people on my team simply gave up – it was just all too hard. Too hard to find customers, too hard to engage people, too hard to stay positive. But I didn't want to be that person, I stayed positive, motivated and I pushed myself harder, mainly to be a good example as a leader.

Leading my team from the other side of the world with an army of women who felt connected to me through social media hadn't always been easy, but now it had become even harder. I worked 50-60 hours a week to empower them on a daily basis and set them up for great success. When you care about people and make them feel good about themselves, support them, help them to believe in themselves, they get attached to you, they trust you, they love you, and they look up to you. My biggest intention in this business is to show women what potential they have, make them believe that they are enough and show them that there is so much more strength and power inside them. Even in tough times like that, you grow even more. Leaders are built through challenges and struggles. I love to uplift people and validate them for their actions, because I know how amazing that feels. When someone believes in you more than you believe in yourself and shows you how incredible you are, you get one step closer to being stronger and gaining confidence. You can only succeed in this business if you believe in yourself.

When times get tough you really get to see who is made for this business. I lost a few leaders along the way, which was devastating. I had poured my heart and soul into them and their businesses and supported them throughout the years to change their lives. I believed in them so strongly and saw such amazing careers ahead of them. I really learned to let go of people that didn't believe in the mission and vision like I did. People that I thought were my friends and were there for the sisterhood. But when money and challenges come into the game, you quickly begin to see a different side to some people. It was a big learning curve for me.

There were times when I spent all day with the boys, trying to keep them away from my husband, so he could do his job. I often didn't get anything done for my business and I set my alarm for 5.30am in the mornings, went for a run and tried to get some work in before everyone woke up. I just wanted to keep everyone happy and I held my own needs back. I mean what did I really need? Nothing. I felt complete with everything I had and I was grateful for it every single day.

Stephanie didn't cope well with the lockdowns; she missed travelling as much as I did and we even got closer during this challenging time. I used my morning runs to listen to her voice messages. Hearing her voice really made me happy, she was the only one who I felt actually understood me.

Learning to lead in such negative circumstances was taxing. I tried with all my might to keep my team motivated. I showed up no matter how I felt and tried to be their rock during this time. I believed that we would rally, and that the world would go back to normal in a month or so. But, as we all know, the entire pandemic crisis took way longer than anyone had anticipated.

When it comes to leadership, I find that your own motivation impacts your whole team, if the leader is not motivated, they sense it. I remember many times when I woke up in the morning and felt like a failure, someone who just couldn't get it right, didn't feel enough and doubted myself. That's all part of the journey, but when you let yourself go and stick to that feeling, you won't be able to bring excitement across to your team. They sense your demotivation, they feel your struggle, they let go of their dreams, because they think, if she can't do it, I can't do it. You don't want it to come to this, you want your team up and running, feeling inspired by you. So, this was a time for me to really knock my leadership out of the park.

Things with my husband were charged and tense. It was almost like he'd saved up all his frustrations with me over the years just for that time we were stuck at home together. There were so many petty things that irritated him – I packed the dishwasher wrong, or the way I folded the towels caused a tantrum. He also pretended to be funny while making derogatory comments about my body. An emotional trigger that only he knew how to set off. Also probably not the best thing to say to someone who had battled and recovered from an eating disorder. He'd 'jokingly' squeeze my tummy and say, "Oh you really enjoyed your food, hey." I'd leave the butter out of the fridge and he'd have a fit. It was awful and hurtful. But I didn't have the energy or any ideas about how to make it right. All my time was spent either trying to keep the boys quiet while he was in meetings, or interacting with my team to try to keep them going. But it all just didn't seem to be enough.

It was only at the end of May when things began to open up again that I was able to have my breast augmentation – by then I really felt I needed the confidence boost. I felt battered and run-down from the relentless negativity from my husband and from the unravelling of the successful team I had built. Of course, the pandemic caused so much more than relationship struggles and business failures. There was so much devastation and loss of life. It left an indelible mark on so many lives.

One morning during the pandemic, I woke up early as usual to go for my run. In the middle of my running track, I found a playing card – the Ace of Hearts. I used to find playing cards in random places all the time, but never paid them much attention, until this specific morning. I stopped to pick it up and instantly began to smile. In that very moment, I just knew that something was about to happen that would absolutely change my life. I was absolutely clueless as to what it would be, but I was right.

The Ace of Hearts card I picked up

The Ace of Hearts is often referred to as the "ace of love" is linked to unconditional love, emotional stability and new beginnings. If you're spiritual and pull this card during a reading, it can mean a rekindling of old flames, a deep spiritual connection, or a birth or new beginning.

I didn't know it at the time, but I was about to embark on my very own new beginning.

INTROSPECTION

COVID impacted everyone in some way – and I'm pretty sure we still don't really understand the implications. So much loss.

1. Have you ever experienced the rollercoaster of immense success followed by a sudden loss of everything? Reflect on how that journey has shaped you and your resilience. How can you find new meaning and purpose in the face of such adversity, using your inner strength to rebuild and redefine your path?

2. When you have reached the pinnacle of success only to have it all come crashing down, how can you find the resilience to rise again? Reflect on your past achievements and the lessons learned from your failures. How can you channel your inner strength and determination to rebuild your life and pursue new paths towards success and fulfilment?

3. When you begin to sense that your relationship is breaking down, what emotions and thoughts arise within you? Take a moment to acknowledge and explore those feelings. How can you proactively address the issues at hand and initiate

open and honest communication with your partner? In what ways can you prioritise self-reflection and seek support to navigate this challenging situation, with the intention of fostering understanding, growth, and the potential for healing in your relationship?

CHAPTER TEN | MESSING UP

"You should never be ashamed to admit you have been wrong. It only proves you are wiser today than yesterday."
— Jonathan Swift

As the world opened up again, I was hopeful that I could get my team back on track. I could get out of the house again. I was so looking forward to spending time with friends and doing 'normal' things. Of course, the world was still strange and very different, but at least we were no longer cooped up inside, not knowing what was going to happen next.

Elective surgeries were taking place again and I was able to go ahead with my breast augmentation. In true German-style, I was really early for my pre-surgery consultation with my surgeon. Normally my husband would have joined me, but he was stuck in meetings that day. I had to make my way there on my own, feeling so anxious. I didn't like it at all. I went into a nearby cafe for a coffee while I waited for the time to pass and to try to calm my nerves.
I was excited but nervous; despite the fact that the surgery had been delayed only because of COVID, I still had remnants of fear

that something was wrong with me that would delay surgery again. A man sat at the table next to me and out of nowhere asked me if I was okay. Was my nervousness and anxiety really that apparent?

When I looked up, I saw a truly kind face. Not a handsome face by any means, but one that showed such incredible compassion and genuine care. The man asked me if he could get me another coffee, but I declined. I thought it was quite funny that he picked up on my mood and joked that maybe I should have said yes to the coffee offer, just to look a bit more put together. We both laughed and continued with a bit of small talk and I mentioned that I was about to meet with my surgeon.

He was incredibly reassuring, telling me that this was the best hospital with the best doctors and medical support, and that I had nothing to worry about. He worked nearby and knew the hospital quite well. When I was leaving to go to my appointment, he handed me his card, saying "By the way, my name is Mike. Reach out if you need another pep talk before your surgery." I looked at his card and saw he was a really high-profile professional.

I felt so much calmer after talking to him. For the first time in a long while, I felt like someone truly cared about my feelings and was genuinely interested in how I felt. It was a new kind of validation for me.

My appointment went really well and my surgeon was amazing. I was good to go for my surgery the following week. I couldn't have been more excited. Finally, it was going to happen. My body, mind and soul were ready and I felt so strong, fit and healthy. I knew it was going to be a great experience, and of course I was hoping to recover quickly. The man I'd met at the coffee shop kept crossing my mind during the week that followed. I couldn't stop thinking about him and his kindness towards me. He had this warm, caring, funny side to him that had really calmed me down that day.

Operation day was finally here and I had to go in alone again since COVID restrictions in the hospital meant that my husband was not allowed to come with me. Despite the difficulties we'd been going through, I still relied on him to be with me in such circumstances, and as a result I was very anxious. He just dropped me off and would pick me up again when I was done. I felt like little Mel again left in the back row of the school bus, scared and anxious. Even though I really wanted the surgery and I felt confident and strong, I somehow still felt lost. I just wanted someone to give me a hug and tell me that I wasn't going to die.

I arrived at the hospital at 6:45am and I was scheduled to be in the theatre at 8am. I had to take my nail polish off, no makeup or cream on my face, and remove my belly piercing. I felt like the ugliest little duckling. As I walked through the front door I heard a familiar, calming voice coming from one of the passageways. I walked towards the voice and was surprised to see the friendly man from the cafe. What was he doing here?

Before I had a second to think about what I looked like, he'd recognised me and smiled. "It's YOU! Is today your big day? Are you ready?" I managed a quiet and shy, "Yes, ready to get it done." I just knew he could feel my angst. He touched my arm with his warm soft fingers and said with a wink: "Trust me, you'll be ok, I promise you. You have my card, let me know how you go."

At that moment, I just wanted to fall into his arms and cry like a little kid. I felt so alone. How bizarre that you can have two unmedicated, natural births and severe pain for hours, but stress your brains out over a forty-five minute procedure that you sleep through the whole time. It was new territory for me.

I got changed into my hospital gown (which was open in the back), a little surgery cap and some blue plastic hospital slippers. As a fashion-lover, I looked ridiculous! Imagine if Mike had seen me like this? What was he doing in the hospital anyway? I never did find out, but I was glad to have bumped into him again to calm my nerves.

The surgery went extremely well, and I was sent home with so much medication. I have never really been a person that takes any kind of medication so it made me quite nervous. I wasn't allowed to walk around for at least two days and luckily, our au pair was able to take the boys to school and entertain them in the afternoons. I made myself comfortable in my bed and I actually liked having an excuse to do nothing for a change. Since my job allowed me to work from anywhere, I could stay on top of it all from the comfort of my bed.

I still thought about the nice man from the cafe, Mike, and our awkward encounter right before my surgery. He just made me feel safe. I remembered the card he gave me, pulled it out of my purse and messaged him to say that the operation went well and that I'm still alive. He didn't reply straight away, so I figured he was busy with work.

A few days later, I felt more myself but I was still trying to manage all the medications. I wasn't in much pain and wanted to avoid the painkillers and some other stuff that I had already forgotten what it was for. Mike messaged me back and asked me how I was coping. I have no idea why it made my heart jump, to see his message, maybe it was all the medication. I told him how I was feeling and he was so calming and helped relieve my nerves.

We messaged a bit back and forth and I I told him how helpful the pharmacist was and that I was so grateful for his reassurance when I was feeling out of sorts. His response was, "Of course the pharmacist was helpful to such a beautiful, stunning woman." I was dumbfounded and a little excited too. I mean, he's seen me in the rawest state that I can be, right?

It's difficult to explain how it felt – I felt good though. I couldn't remember the last time my husband told me that I was beautiful.

A week later he messaged me and said he was off to Melbourne and was thinking about moving there. I realised that I didn't want him to go. How weird was that? I mean, what was I doing here? And then I did something that still shocks me to this day – I asked him if he would like to meet up for a coffee at his favourite cafe when he returned from his trip. My heart was thumping, but something inside of me was drawing me towards him and wanted to see him again. I will never forget the moment I typed that message. I felt hot and cold and it all felt so wrong, but it all felt so right, too. Did I really just ask another man out to have a coffee with me? It did not make any sense at the time, but a year later the puzzle pieces came together for me. The universe truly guided me.

My phone popped up with a message and he said, "Why would I say no to this? Would love to see you again."

I was sleeping in Lui's bed the first couple of weeks after my operation, while the boys slept in the master bedroom with my husband. So, I was alone at night and this became the time when Mike and I communicated for hours on end. We spoke about everything and through it all, he was so supportive and sweet to me.

My husband was also incredibly supportive then – he would help me out of bed in the mornings and make sure that I had everything I needed. He made sure the boys understood why I couldn't give them big hugs, and he was generally very courteous and caring. That's why my excitement about Mike didn't make much sense. But I guess because of the previous months and years of us growing apart, I was able to separate it from my real life.

My interactions with Mike made me realise that this was something I wasn't getting from my husband. While we'd been living the good life, we had also been living past each other. Even though it was something I knew deep down, I hadn't wanted to admit to myself that my marriage wasn't working. We weren't on the same page anymore – somehow, we'd grown apart and it didn't seem like we even wanted each other anymore. We certainly didn't have an intimate relationship and while we were living large, it was mostly about the boys. When we weren't together as a family, we were just focussed on work.

When Mike returned from his trip, we met up for lunch at a lovely restaurant. That lunch turned into an afternoon of the most delicious conversation and a bit of flirting. I could not remember the last time I had felt so carefree and happy. I was laughing, I felt seen, I felt heard and appreciated. During the whole lunch, he didn't look at his phone – he paid me so much attention. He really listened to me and every few minutes he told me how beautiful I was and how strong and interesting I was. I was on cloud nine.

This was so unlike me – I'm an incredibly loyal person and have never before even looked at another man. I've never even flirted before. Going out with my girlfriends, they always commented on the men that looked at me and it didn't ever occur to me to look back. I was married and that was that. So, this interaction with Mike was completely out of character for me.

The next day during my morning run, I told Stephanie about him. I cried, because I felt ashamed. I didn't want this to happen at all, but it somehow did. I asked her to not judge me and I told her the whole story – how wonderful this man was, how he made me feel and that I thought I had a crush on him. Stephanie's immediate response was that she didn't realise that I was having issues in my marriage and went on to ask a million questions, mostly about me and my husband. I told her about the issues we'd had during the lockdown and how he had tantrums every other day because of something I'd done or not done. I'd never told her about that before. I was protective towards him, despite his behaviour – the same way I protected her and made excuses for her behaviour on the incentive trip. Stephanie had always been very open about her relationship with her husband and I knew things weren't all that great – in fact, she'd had an affair. I remember asking her at the time who the person was, and I asked her again then, but she always maintained that it was just some random guy.

I simply had to share my excitement about this man and how I was feeling because I couldn't remember feeling like that before, even with my husband. She turned out to be very supportive towards me and my feelings for Mike. We chatted constantly, like two school girls with a crush, and I was so happy she didn't judge me. She was, in fact, very much on my side and questioned if my husband was the right man for me after all.

I started to really believe that I had strong feelings for Mike and because of my loyal nature, it was never going to be a sordid affair. I was fantasising about us leaving our respective spouses and being together. It was ridiculous, of course. I didn't express any of this to him, and we continued to message almost every day.

As things were opening up in the world again, my husband and I got back into the routine of not seeing much of each other. Of course, we saw each other in the mornings and evenings, but our days were filled with work and he was out and about for work at least twice a week. Our weekends were still all about the boys and we did many things together as a family. Back to normal. But I had this secret – this man that was constantly telling me how gorgeous and clever and amazing I was. I am surprised that nobody noticed the new glow in me, the new bounce in my step. Maybe my husband thought it was just because of my new boobs?

If my husband made any move to reignite our intimacy, I'd never have known because all my heart was taken up with speaking to Mike. I felt more disconnected from my husband and I started seeing a lot of red flags that I have never seen in him before. Stephanie and I became closer than ever. Every morning when I woke up, I had voice messages from her and she wanted to know what was going on with me and my husband. She was rather perturbed about what was going on with him, and not so much Mike. Did I want to leave my husband? Or what was my plan?

I couldn't answer her questions. I felt terrible talking to another guy, but at the same time I felt so uplifted when we spoke. I told Stephanie that I wanted to see him again so badly, but it wouldn't be a good idea. She told me if I didn't go see him then I would never find out if he is the right man for me or not. Even though I'd seen him physically only three times – once when we met in the coffee shop, once just before my surgery, and once when we went out for lunch, we communicated quite often; but I also knew that he had such a demanding job that a relationship between us would never work. Nevermind that I didn't even know this person. What was I thinking?

A few days later I had a massive disagreement with my husband. Once again, I didn't hang up the towels properly in the bathroom and the dishwasher wasn't sorted the way he wanted it to be. He got very angry and yelled at me in front of the boys. I had no strength left to make everything right for him, so I just turned around and went upstairs. I cried in the bathroom and asked myself, "What are you doing Mel? You are living with a man who constantly criticises you and has no nice words to say anymore." I was seeing it more and more, how my husband was treating me disrespectfully in front of our friends, and our au pair. When we were out with the children, he didn't hold my hand anymore. He complained in the mornings when I was doing my team meetings and live events. We weren't sitting together at the pool on the weekends or just having coffee and chatting like we always did. We didn't have any deep conversations anymore. He seemed angry and stressed every day and the only time he tried to be funny was when he was making fun of me. I realised I wasn't happy anymore at all. Mike popped into my mind and that was the moment I decided to see him again. Stephanie agreed to my plan and she was angry at my husband for treating me like that. She encouraged me, saying I deserved better.

That night my husband and I went to bed without talking to each other. I could feel his frustration with me; he wanted me to do things that I didn't see as important. There was always more coming to top it off, too. The way I cooked, the way I said things, just was never enough for him. Talking disrespectfully in front of the children is a no-go for me and it made me especially upset that night.

It wasn't unusual for me to go out in the evenings without my husband – we both had busy schedules and he knew that in my business, networking was vital. I also had regular girls' nights out, so when I was getting ready that night, there was no suspicion from him. When I got to the bar where I was meeting Mike, I got a message from Stephanie. She seemed super nervous for me but excited at the same time. She always told me to delete all the messages between us, just in case my husband would ever listen to them. At one point I thought that was strange because my husband would never look at my phone; he trusted me. I wouldn't look at his phone either. He had even said to me once that I was too stupid to even flirt with someone; that hurt. The fact was that I never wanted to flirt with anyone other than him, which is what made me even more upset. Stephanie cared about me, she knew that I needed to make a decision soon, she knew this wasn't me and I could not do this any longer. I rang her quickly, she wished me good luck and said that she would always support me in any decision I made.

When he arrived at the bar thirty minutes late, it was already dark outside. A message from my husband popped up on my phone asking where I was. It confused me, as I had told him that I was out with a friend. We ordered a drink and some food and Mike complimented me on my cute dress, which fit perfectly and looked amazing thanks to my new boobs. My phone rang the minute our drinks arrived and I saw it was my husband. He kept calling until I picked up. He yelled through the phone that he knew where I was and that I was with another man. He was furious. My heart dropped and I felt my whole world falling apart. All I could say was, "I'm coming home." I stood up and looked at Mike and said, "I have to go, he found out, I'm sorry."

I ran as fast as I could out of the bar, not even remembering my own name, where I'd parked and how I would get home. Everything was a blur. I stood in front of the elevator that took me down to the carpark and as soon as the door opened, I noticed Mike standing behind me; he had run all the way after me. He looked worried and completely confused. I stepped into the lift and just shook my head and whispered, "I'm sorry, I need to fix this." The doors closed and I fell on the ground.

It took me half a lifetime to drive home, because I couldn't find my credit card to pay for the parking and I got lost in the city, all while I was crying and worrying. All I wanted, in that moment, was to apologise to my husband. I knew how devastated and shocked he was. While I was driving I received a message from Stephanie asking how my night was. It was a bit weird that she'd messaged to check on me so soon after we'd chatted while I was at the bar. I managed to ring her and just cried on the phone telling her that my husband found out and I'd left Mike just standing there at the lift. She was confused. How could he find out? She asked me straight away if I deleted every conversation with him. I hadn't. I explained to her that they made me feel good. When I felt down, I would read his words – they were comforting. She said, "You need to delete everything Mel, get rid of everything!"

By the time I got home he had made up a bed for himself on the couch. I was crying and begging him to listen to me. I wanted to open up and explain what was going on. He didn't want to listen. He was completely heartbroken, angry and I couldn't talk to him. We both didn't sleep that night.

The next morning he didn't speak to me at all and left early for work. I was in the kitchen making coffee and breakfast for the boys when our au pair walked in. She just looked at me and asked if I was alright, because she had noticed him sleeping on the couch. I broke down crying and said, "I have done something really bad and I need to fix this." She hugged me and said that I could talk to her anytime to get it off my chest.

Our au pair and I were very close, so I told her everything later when the kids were at school. Stephanie tried to call me all day, but I just didn't want to talk. I was ashamed and I felt like the worst person in the world. I needed to sort it out. I told her that I needed some time to work on my marriage and she was shocked by that decision. I got the feeling that she didn't want my marriage to work out – maybe she was just projecting her own unsettled marriage onto me. I admitted that I'd made a mistake and I would do anything to explain and make it right again. He did not deserve this. I was selfish and attention-driven and I regretted every conversation I ever had with Mike. It was all so wrong.

I begged him all day to sit down with me at dinner and talk about it. We ended up going to a Mexican restaurant and I told him that I was sorry and I messed up. I explained that I was not happy in our marriage, that I didn't feel supported or respected and I slipped into something completely ridiculous. I can't remember everything we talked about that night, but we said it all. Well, at least I said it all, and at the time I believed that he opened up to me fully as well.

He told me that he'd seen all the messages on my laptop – I'd forgotten that everything was linked. He knew everything. Why hadn't I listened to Stephanie when she told me to delete all the conversations? Had *she* told him to go look at my messages? The question was gone as soon as it entered my mind. Stephanie wouldn't do that to me, she was my best friend. Besides, she was so supportive of me meeting up with Mike again.

It felt good to let it all out though. I had held back so much over the last few years and ignored so many red flags. I had never told him the things that I was missing in our marriage. For the first time, I opened up to him and told him that I wasn't really happy. He opened up too, telling me that he wasn't happy either. He felt like I wasn't listening to him, especially when he asked me to fold the towels a certain way and pack the dishwasher the way he liked. I had made him feel like I didn't care about those things and how he liked them.

I explained that we had three options: either I move out and we end our relationship, we try to fix it and work through this, or we give it a break for a few months. Straight away he said that he wanted to work through it. Great! Me too.

INTROSPECTION

I guess that we all have moments when we could flirt with someone other than our partner – and we have a choice in that moment. There is no way that any indiscretion is not a decision; but sometimes it's hard to make the right decision. A split second can change everything.

1. When you've made a serious mistake or hurt someone you deeply care about in a relationship, how do you confront your own actions and take responsibility? Reflect on the importance of accountability and acknowledging the impact of your actions on your partner. How can you actively work towards rebuilding trust and demonstrating genuine remorse to nurture the potential for reconciliation and healing in your relationship?

2. How do you handle the overwhelming feelings of guilt and regret when you've jeopardised an important relationship? Take a moment to explore the weight of these emotions and their impact on your well-being. How can you practise self-compassion and forgiveness, both towards yourself and others, as you seek to mend the fractures and rebuild the bond with your loved one?

3. When facing the consequences of a major relationship mistake, how do you prevent yourself from spiralling into negativity and self-doubt? Reflect on strategies that can help you maintain a positive mindset and keep moving forward. How can you draw strength from past challenges you've

overcome to empower yourself to confront this situation with determination and a growth-oriented outlook?

4. How do you navigate the complexities of rebuilding trust after a serious relationship setback? Reflect on the steps you can take to demonstrate genuine change and commitment to your partner's emotional well-being. How can open communication, empathy, and consistency in your actions contribute to the process of healing and rebuilding a stronger, more resilient relationship?

CHAPTER ELEVEN | CRASH LANDINGS

"Our greatest glory is not in never falling, but in rising every time we fall"
– Confucius.

For a while we tip-toed around each other, both feeling sensitive and nervous. I could see that my husband was trying, and believe me, I was trying too. I was extremely careful to do all the little things that I knew annoyed him just right – like the way I folded towels. We spoke gently to each other and for a while it was quite peaceful.

I still felt like the worst person ever. I was embarrassed at my behaviour. I couldn't believe I had almost sacrificed my marriage. I realised that I didn't want to run away; it was a big wakeup call actually. My husband assumed that I had had a major affair with Mike, which I clearly hadn't. Even though I'd only known Mike for a mere six weeks and we saw each other less than a handful of times, it did feel longer because we shared so much during our chats.

My husband wouldn't let up – he wanted all the details. He kept asking where he was now, was I in love with him, what exactly happened? Every day we had conversations about him. He just could not let it go. He said that no high-profile professional on this earth would ever be in love with me. He would not be serious about me and he would never leave his wife, that he was only playing with me and that he was probably doing the same thing with multiple other girls out there. He said he wanted to protect me from those sorts of men. He insisted on seeing that I had indeed blocked Mike on my phone. And even when I showed him, he didn't believe me. There were never any messages from Mike because he didn't message me after that night at the bar – I'm pretty sure my quick explanation as I was rushing away scared him. Too messy, I guess.

When I woke up in the morning after our dinner, my husband was sitting right next to me on the edge of the bed and asked if he were to look at my phone now, would he find any messages from Mike. He wanted to see it with his own eyes, before I even got the chance to delete anything. This went on for about three weeks; it was incredibly hard to deal with. Three weeks was half the time I'd known Mike. Whenever I was on or near my phone, which was quite a lot because of my work, my husband asked if I was messaging him again. He started to doubt all the events I'd been to and coffee dates with team members or mum's group catch-ups. He questioned every single little thing.

Every step felt like it was controlled. I was walking on eggshells. He installed cameras inside and outside the house, saying that it was because of a spate of burglaries in the area. But it really felt like he just wanted to be able to constantly check up on me, especially when he was not home. If I went for a run and happened to be on my phone as I was returning, he'd see that and accuse me of speaking to Mike. I remember going to buy the boys new school shoes and strolling around the mall for an hour or two afterwards, so it took me longer than he had expected. When I got home, he checked the receipt's timestamp, and demanded to know what I had been doing all that time. I didn't have any later receipts because I hadn't actually bought anything – so he didn't believe me at all. Every week I joined an outside boot camp and one day when I got home he said I wasn't sweating, so I must have been lying about where I was. If I didn't come back from grocery shopping after thirty minutes, he would video call me just to check that I was where I said I was going.

One night I woke up with severe vertigo. It felt like I was spinning around like crazy and I couldn't stop that feeling for about thirty seconds. I nearly threw up. Since that night I pretty much experienced vertigo attacks on a daily basis. I was woken up by them. During the day I couldn't tilt my head back at all or I would lose balance. I got my ears checked, my blood checked, no one could find anything wrong with me. My vertigo attacks got worse and worse and I struggled to work out. A really good friend of mine told me that it was because my soul was out of balance. That really hit me.

It all eventually got too much for me. I spoke to my sister and Stephanie, and neither of them could believe the intensity of his behaviour. One day, I was out by the pool sunbathing and took a few selfies to post on social media and he could see me through the window. He rushed outside and asked what I was doing – he thought I was taking pictures to send to Mike. He was constantly observing me through the window, making sure I wasn't on my phone, or taking photos. I felt so insecure about even touching my phone or working on my computer, because whenever I did, he never believed I was actually working. It made it so hard to stay in contact with my team, my girlfriends, my customers – the people that I uplifted every single day through messages, emails and social media. It was a never-ending cycle and I constantly tried to think of ways to get out of it. How could I possibly prove to him that I was still trying to build my empire, that I was earning money, worrying about other women and worrying about my business crashing down, because I couldn't be the person that I was anymore?

I needed a break. The stress of being scrutinised at every moment of my life was too much to bear. One of my girlfriends said that his behaviour was so over the top and that it sounded like he was the one having an affair. Of course, anyone would get upset and suspicious if they thought their spouse was cheating, but my husband was going beyond an appropriate response. I brushed that idea off – I defended him, despite the fact that he liked to flirt. I trusted him more than anything.

My girlfriends started questioning why I wasn't going out with them anymore, and why I had been so reserved. If I met up with a friend for a coffee, I always made sure I took a selfie with her and sent it to him, so he knew that I was not out with someone else. I mean what more could I do? I felt sorry and ashamed, as well as drained, sad, lonely, misunderstood and not respected at all. How did I get into this situation? I thought more and more about the idea of getting marriage counselling, but one point really held me back; he did not seem to make an effort anymore. All he talked about was Mike and how I could cheat and that he wanted to know what happened but then didn't believe a word I said. How could I ever make this right?

My breast augmentation gave me so much confidence that I finally felt complete in my body. But the rest of my life was all over the place. I guess you can't have it all, right? My business was still struggling. I was trying to keep leaders motivated and saw so many people dropping off even after COVID, because they simply didn't have the strength to power through. I knew that my leadership skills would only get better if I could remain a smiling face through this period. I knew the only way to survive was keep going. I was going through so much pain and I had to hide it all from the public.

Being positive in a negative situation is not naïve, it's leadership.

The fun part about having my new boobs was my experience with different fashion items and going shopping for new tops and dresses. I didn't hide my surgery on social media, I wanted to still be authentic and empower women out there to do what feels good to them. Since I had struggled pretty much all my life with body issues, it just felt wrong hiding a plastic surgery. I will never forget the day I walked into a bra store and said, "I'm looking to buy some bras, can you help me find my size?" It felt amazing! I'd never really worn bras before, because I just didn't need to. I got home with four new bras and it was a whole new experience for me. Would I be one of those women who buys pretty bras on a monthly basis in different colours and styles now? I wouldn't think so, but hey, here I was with my new bra collection and I was so excited to try them on and feel feminine.

Coming home from my successful bra shopping day, I ran upstairs and told my husband I was going to have a quick shower. I wanted to surprise him that night with my new things. I hoped that we could just go to bed without him asking questions again about Mike or me being unfaithful for a change. I was hoping for peace, for sanity, I wanted this drama to come to an end.

Before getting into the shower, I decided to try them on again – I stood in front of the mirror and I felt great. I felt empowered and so happy with my body. I was so focused on falling in love with my new bras and accepting my body as a whole, I didn't hear him come into the bathroom. He immediately accused me of sending nudes to Mike and made a big scene, saying I bought the lingerie for him. The suspicion and anger were relentless. All my excitement was gone within a second. I just wanted to cry; would this ever end? Deep down I longed for Mike, he gave me so much more. Why was I stuck in this and why wouldn't my husband see that I was trying to make this right? I felt ashamed and awful again. This night ended as pretty much every other night ended. He asked a thousand questions, accused me of lying to him, more arguments and discussions, hectic conversations, going around in circles, not getting anywhere with our words and emotions and me crying myself to sleep, or leaving the bedroom and sleeping on the couch. Exhausted.

My sister told me that I needed to leave, so that I could have a break. She said it was just too fresh for him and too frustrating. I felt like he was pushing me back into the arms of Mike because when my husband was behaving like a madman, all I could think of was the quiet reassurance and peace I felt when I was with him.

I did message him once, but he didn't respond. I was devastated because I felt like I'd lost everything and that I was close to losing my sanity as well. The vertigo attacks got more frequent and I had several during the day. My personal trainer had to change my exercise routine and set up different stations for me, because I could not lay down flat without my head being elevated.

I couldn't go out with my girlfriends, because it would have caused so much trouble. I didn't have the strength anymore to constantly explain, so I turned down every invitation to go anywhere. On top of being under surveillance all the time, I also felt trapped. Stephanie had also encouraged me to get away for a bit. She reminded me of her affair and said her husband had acted in a similar way when it all came out. I didn't remember her talking about him behaving quite as intensely, but I agreed. She said that the only other option was therapy, but that he and I would both have to open up about everything and that wasn't something she thought I would want. Why not? I'd already shared my whole side of the story. What more could I say?

I eventually told my husband that I needed a break. I just wanted a couple of months on my own. He completely freaked out, so I left the idea. But not long after, I broke down and begged him to let me go – I was on the edge of a nervous breakdown. He was treating me so poorly; it seemed like he wanted to punish me for what I'd done and didn't seem to realise that I was trying my best to make it right again. I told him that I could fly to Sydney and stay with a friend for a few days. Surprisingly, he agreed to that, even telling me to book into a nice hotel and spoil myself. I jumped at it and immediately booked my flights and hotel. But it wasn't the break I needed.

Almost the minute I landed, the phone calls and accusations began. He accused me of being there with Mike. He seemed to obsessively check my social media and one picture of two glasses of wine with a glass of water made him so angry – he thought that the third glass belonged to Mike. I felt anxious every time I heard my phone go off. He video called me all the time, and if I didn't answer the phone, he bombarded me with accusations. I just wanted to disappear, I wanted to run away. It felt like it would never end. What a mess I'd made in our marriage.

It didn't let up when I returned either. It was two months of hell. I thought about Mike more and more, and started to doubt that my husband's behaviour would ever change and that we would ever be able to work through the insanity of it all. In September, I rented an apartment for two weeks, telling the boys that I needed extra space to work.

I had to get away from him, even if it broke us completely. We couldn't communicate with each other anymore, everything turned into accusations. It got worse and worse every day. I was preparing my team for a big month in November and I needed a clear head and strong mindset to pull it off.

I still thought about Mike and since I was feeling so powerless, stressed, disrespected and lonely, I reached out to him to see if he wanted to chat. Much to my surprise, he responded. He came and picked me up and we went for a drive. I needed to see him and hear his voice. It felt good. We parked and I told him what I had been going through; he was holding my hand and told me that he'd missed me. And then he leaned in to kiss me. I could tell he wanted more in that moment, but that's not what I wanted and I asked him to drive me back home. It felt nice to just relax for a second and have someone next to me who adored me. But did he really? It felt like he was more interested in my body than anything else, which made me feel confused. I was longing for this deep conversation, someone to laugh with, someone I can feel safe with, someone who sees my heart, my soul, my mind and not just my outside. When we arrived back at my place, he wanted to come up with me but I refused.

I rang Stephanie straight away and told her that he wanted more than just to talk. Obviously. I would have never gone that far, she knew that. I missed our chats and his caring character, I wasn't drawn to him in a physical way at all. Stephanie told me that I was naïve to think that he wasn't going to try to sleep with me.

My husband called all the time saying he wanted me back. He said that if I stayed away, it would show that I didn't love him anymore. Those two weeks didn't help either – I was working hard, doing Zoom calls every night and fielding angry calls and texts from my husband the rest of the time. Trying to hide my sorrows and feelings in front of my team and pouring all the energy that I had left into them. I kept a happy face on social media. No one would have ever thought that I felt completely torn on the inside. I loved my husband and I wanted to make it work, so, I packed up and went home. I wanted to show him that I'll be there when he needs me. That I wanted to work through this. I wanted to fight for our family.

Everyone deals with such situations differently. But I suddenly remembered that December when I saw the text from another woman on his phone while we were engaged; and how I just pushed it aside. I guess when you've done something wrong and feel such guilt about it, thoughts of the other person also doing wrong seem to surface. But as those thoughts floated to the surface, I pushed them down again. What had I been thinking? Mike wasn't ever going to be the love of my life – my husband was! I'd always believed that and was so astounded that we had arrived at such a dreadful place in our relationship. I was desperate to make it right again.

For my husband it was a massive wake up call. He was so sure of me and my love that he never had to make an effort. I never complained, I always put my needs to the side, because I knew deep down, he loved me.

During the rest of September and October, he really turned around. For the first time, I could actually see that he was making an effort without blaming me for everything – he'd message me during the day to tell me my eyes were beautiful, or that he loved me. It was strange because it wasn't how we'd ever been before, but I really felt like we had turned a corner and that I was falling in love with him again. I cooked for him, brought him breakfast in bed and tried to do everything right. Parking the car properly in the garage, making sure I stayed on top of the laundry and housework, entertaining the kids away from him so he could work uninterrupted. He made me tea and ran a bath for me. He brought home dinner and bought me presents. We were intimate again, we connected on a good level. I told Stephanie that I felt like we were progressing at last and that I saw a side of him that I didn't even know before.

Towards the end of October, I took a friend of mine to stay at a hotel that I'd booked for an event that had been cancelled due to COVID. I hadn't cancelled the booking so I thought it would be fun to have a girls night on the town. Of course, this raised doubts and accusations again and he wasn't at all happy about me going. At that point I wanted to help out my friend as well who had struggled a bit with her business and motivation, and a night of girl time would do wonders for both of us. I needed to get out of the house since I still wasn't going out at all and still cancelled plans with all my girlfriends. The minute I told him, I could see his mood drop. He did not want me to go and it all started again…

That night we had yet another argument about me spending time with my friend and I was very close to calling the whole thing off. After putting the boys to bed, I went to bed early feeling lonely and trapped. I thought about all those times when I was happy and dreaming about all the things I wanted to achieve, my goals, dreams, my life as a family. I had lost my motivation, my mojo, and I decided that night when I cried myself to sleep once again, that I needed to do something for myself.

I wondered what the universe was trying to teach me here. My husband seemed distant again, not caring about anything that was going on with me. My business was full-on and I struggled to keep calm. I still longed for interaction with Mike, even though I knew he just wanted to have sex with me. Could it get any worse?

The next morning I decided it was time to do something to get myself out of this funk, so I did some research on studying to be a stylist. It had always been a dream of mine. My passion for style and fashion could finally become my reality. I signed up to study online as a personal stylist and virtual stylist with one of the best institutes in Australia. I was so excited! The next few weeks I threw myself into online study. I spent hours reading, doing assignments and watching online training. I loved every second of it. I finally felt the power inside of me coming back to life. I had several calls with the leading stylists and set up my own brand, styling ideas and figured out how I would forge ahead with this new experience. This distraction was the best thing that could happen to me in this season of my life. I created a new vision board and started taking out clients for styling experiences, wardrobe edits and shopping trips.

Then it happened again – I found two more playing cards on my morning run. Someone had probably lost an entire card stash somewhere along my running track and the rest were flying around elsewhere. But on that particular day, I believe these cards – the King of Clubs and the Two of Clubs – were a sign that I needed, sent to me from heaven.

The King of Clubs symbolises a dark man who is characterised by his loyalty and kindness. This card is considered a very good omen. On the other hand, the Two of Clubs represents contradiction and hesitation before making an important decision. This card is a sign to take a leap of faith with no rehearsal.

These cards made me think about how they could relate to my life at that moment. A few theories popped into my head but nothing seemed concrete enough to make perfect sense. Maybe I'd see them play out later on in my life?

The Two of Clubs and King of Clubs I picked up on my morning run

My husband still went on every day about me going away with my friend. I wanted to really go and live a normal life again, but I still felt guilty. It frustrated me more than anything that he treated me like a prisoner. I didn't want to feel this way anymore and I got more and more upset about the life we were living as a couple. It was so hard and challenging for me to keep my cool and my motivation for my team high. Pretending that I was ok everyday in front of my children, when I actually wasn't. When I was in meetings with my team or taking clients out to style, I didn't feel judged; I felt me again, I felt appreciated, I felt loved and valued. In my marriage I didn't feel those things at all anymore. But I wasn't giving up. I tried my best every day to make it right for him. I messed up big time and would carry that guilt forever.

The day arrived – my awaited night out with my girlfriend. I couldn't sleep properly days beforehand, because I knew he would go crazy, while I was away. By that time, I just wanted to get out, be me, feel carefree; without him spying on me non-stop, making me feel bad, making me feel more guilty and insecure.

I walked into the hotel bar and my heart started racing, I felt excitement and sadness at the same time. I walked through the hallway and couldn't remember my name, like I was in another world. It was where I'd had that first fateful lunch with Mike. All the memories came flooding back. I hadn't heard from him at all and he was blocked on all my social platforms. I kind of missed him, but kept reminding myself that my husband was the love of my life. I had said yes to *him, he* had brought me to this country and we had a wonderful life with two incredible children. Deep down, I wasn't happy though. I tried to deny it, and I needed to get the selfish thought out of my mind that I wanted more from my relationship.

Walking through that hotel bar with all those feelings coming back up, I thought about what I was going through at home and realised that I never wanted any of this to happen. I suddenly thought about the King of Clubs card that I'd picked up. Was this meant for me? I could only try. I realised years later that this card hasn't played a role in my life yet. But that night, I messaged Mike. Because obviously I'm a sucker for punishment. When I think back, I wish I hadn't. I regret that I still didn't see my worth, but I guess we just go through life and have to learn all those lessons, even if it means learning them the hard way.

Surprisingly, he turned up. There was no doubt that Mike was expecting us to sleep together and he could hardly keep his hands off me. In a bar, with muted lighting, it's easier to get close to someone than at a restaurant in the middle of the day. We kissed. I don't know if I felt anything, but I felt wanted. I really felt wanted. Of course I wasn't planning on going further than that. If I'm going to sleep with someone then I need to be all in, and since we were both married, it wasn't going to happen – we hadn't made that type of commitment to each other.

We had a few drinks before going up to my room. He immediately tried to undress me and I tried to fend him off. Why couldn't I just let it go and move on? Something was up, I could feel it. I knew that he wanted me, but he didn't understand that I wasn't there for sex. I just couldn't. I just didn't want to. Again, I craved the attention and the feeling of being enough. I craved a deep conversation, someone looking at me differently, seeing my true self and enjoying being with me, laughing with me. For a while I thought, that was it, that's what I wanted. But then I quickly realised what was happening – we weren't on the same page. He just didn't stop and I knew that if I wasn't going to get out right now, I would regret this for the rest of my life. So I pushed him off and told him "I don't want this, I'm leaving." I grabbed my stuff, zipped my dress back up and ran out of the hotel room. I cried myself to sleep again that night.

I haven't seen him since.

I was running in circles, I wouldn't learn, would I? My life was a mess and I was in the middle of it all, trying to escape, realising I needed to fix things, but didn't know how. My energy was low, my guilt was deep, my self-esteem crushed.

When you go through phases like this, you seem to be blind to the true meaning of it. What is life trying to teach us here? We have to learn to be happy from the inside and within ourselves in order to let others love us. I was too focused on someone loving me, that I totally forgot how to love myself first.

I called Stephanie the next day to tell her what had happened. Weirdly, she kept pushing me to admit that I had actually slept with him. She shouted at me for being too in control of everything in my life; she didn't understand how I could always have my feelings and actions under control, so much so that I couldn't even let go for a second. There was a part of me that wanted to be like her, sensual and carefree. This was one thing she always accused me of: being too disciplined and always following the rules. I could sense her disappointment in me, that I didn't let go and sleep with him. I felt like she had expected me to do it. She wouldn't let it go. She wanted me to just say it, to admit it, to tell her. I already felt like an absolute failure; towards my marriage, towards Mike, and now towards my best friend as well. As a last-ditch effort to get her off my back and stop calling me a prude, I eventually lied and told her that I had slept with him.

Several months later I discovered why she was so insistent that I admit it. That made her actions very clear to me. And most of all, I regret the fact that I sent that message to her. That one message that changed my whole life.

November came around, and it was the biggest month for our team. I needed full concentration and focus on our team goals and especially on some of my leaders who were going for big promotions. Out of nowhere, Stephanie pulled out – saying that she needed to concentrate on her family. It was so sudden, and she said I wouldn't understand because I didn't value family the way she did – something that was obvious because of my recent behaviour. Our conversations went in a different direction. It was such a strange thing for her to do. Not only was she going to lose out on a great commission, but she was basically saying she didn't approve of my behaviour, after being so encouraging to me to pursue my relationship with Mike.

A lot of things began to fall apart – we missed our November target. I was way too focused on some of my other leaders to help them with their goals, and I completely miscalculated the team sales. I thought we would hit it easily if everyone went through with their promotions. But we didn't; we missed a massive requalifying status by just a few dollars. We had worked towards this the whole year and I was absolutely devastated. I couldn't believe my eyes when I updated my website for that last minute in November. It was done. We were done. My mind was not focused enough. I was carrying all this grief and sorrow in my marriage, that made me feel like a failure as a human being and now I failed my team and in business as well. I cried for three hours straight. But I quickly realised that this 'failure' was one of the best things that could have ever happened to me and my business.

I needed that wake-up call. I needed something in my business to teach me to stay focused until the end. I poured all my love, time, energy and tears into my leaders and they all hit their goals, and at the end of the day, that's all that mattered to me. If you want to be a great leader you need to step back and let others shine, and you lift them up to a level where they are becoming the best version of themselves. That's always been my goal and always will be. My reputation in the business was really growing. This wasn't a failure; it was a learning curve and it was empowering. I showed up the next day, wiped my tears away and spread the motivation across my international team for the month of December. Last sprint, ladies. Let's do this again!

I'm passionate about leadership and when it comes to being a good leader, you need to be on your team's level. I never saw my team performing better and feeling their motivation through the community more than when I was transparent, vulnerable, and shared emotions and struggles. The connection with my team got stronger each time. People only connect with you when they can relate. Success comes from falling and getting up again. We all have our struggles, no one is perfect, no one gets successful without a struggle, and no one has an easy ride to the top. I showed them how I struggled, but also how I overcame the fear of 'failing', by getting up and starting it all over again. Sharing my feelings and emotions with my team builds trust. I want to create leaders, and inspire women out there to give their best, no matter how it turns out in the end. You gotta try.

It was extremely hot in Brisbane that year and I trained insanely hard to challenge my body, mind and soul. Running was always on top of my priority list. It cleared my head. I came up with the best ideas and it gave me the power and motivation that I needed for the day. I couldn't believe my eyes, when I spied another playing card on the grass along my route. I stopped and looked around me, before picking it up. What's going on? This couldn't be real?

It was the Ace of Clubs.

The Ace of Clubs card I picked up on my morning run

The Ace of Clubs is seen as a symbol of good luck, prosperity and abundance. It represents a signal of good fortune in many cultures and is often associated with success in business or romance. It can also symbolise power and influence.

The timing was perfect.

That December, I poured a hundred percent into our marriage. I booked an amazing holiday for us and the kids in a tropical place and got so excited for a much-needed, overdue vacation.

I really wanted to make it beautiful for us as a family. The boys were really looking forward to it. Unfortunately, it turned out to be an emotional disaster - every time I wore something that was even a little bit revealing, he moaned at me. He was still incredibly suspicious of me, bringing up Mike all the time and accusing me of messaging him, reaching out to him and wishing that he was here with me, instead of him. He couldn't handle when other guys were looking at me and said it was all my fault, because I should dress differently. I mean, we were at a beach resort and literally everyone was running around in swimsuits. I just didn't understand his actions at all. The holiday that I hoped would make a big difference was a complete wash-out. I tried to hide my sadness, disappointment and loneliness in front of the children. I cried behind my sunglasses every day, but put on a happy face for everyone else, just to make sure that it wouldn't escalate. The kids had a ball and didn't sense anything was wrong, but I felt like I was stuck in a situation that was burning my soul.

I was still really upset about Stephanie and didn't understand why she had dropped me so out of the blue. I missed our chats every day, our conversations and everything we shared with each other. I messaged her to wish her a Happy New Year and that I hoped we could reconnect soon. I also sent her flowers and she thanked me for those, but said she didn't want to resume our friendship. I was so confused and her rejection of me really made me question myself. The guilt was never-ending, along with the pressure of my husband's relentless scrutiny wearing me down and making me quite angry.

One evening, I was in the bathroom getting ready for bed when he came in after me, and we had an argument again. He said to me: "Maybe you should take a good look at yourself and your constant actions, since even your best friend doesn't want to have anything to do with you anymore." That cut me deep, and especially so a few months later, when all the cards started playing out on the table.

I was low.

INTROSPECTION

When you've put your all into something and it still doesn't quite get off the ground, all the old insecurities and self-doubt come flooding in – it often doesn't matter if circumstances beyond your control are at play; you still feel at fault.

1. When you've invested your heart and soul into a dream or project, and it fails to take flight, how do you navigate the waves of self-doubt and insecurity that wash over you? Take a moment to contemplate the impact of these feelings on your self-worth and aspirations. How can you cultivate resilience and self-belief amidst the challenges, recognizing that setbacks are part of the journey?

2. When external circumstances seem to conspire against your efforts, and success remains elusive, how can you avoid falling into the trap of self-blame? Reflect on the balance between personal responsibility and acknowledging factors beyond your control. How can practising self-compassion and reframing your perspective empower you to keep moving forward despite the setbacks?

3. What role do past experiences and old insecurities play in amplifying the feelings of fault and self-doubt when faced with adversity? Take a moment to explore how your past might influence your present reactions. How can embracing self-awareness and understanding your triggers help you break free from the cycle of self-blame and foster a more supportive inner dialogue?

4. When pursuing your goals, how can you strike a balance between determination and self-compassion? Reflect on the importance of acknowledging your efforts and progress, even when things don't go as planned. How can celebrating small victories and showing kindness to yourself help you stay motivated and resilient on your journey to success?

CHAPTER TWELVE | UP IN THE AIR

"Every experience, no matter how bad it seems, holds within it a blessing of some kind. The goal is to find it."
– Gauthama The Lord Buddha

We carried on in a sort of truce. He was still going on and on about Mike and he wasn't really being supportive either. I felt like he had dropped me on the floor and was constantly stomping on me.

Early in January the following year, I'd been called to do an interview with some of the other top leaders in the industry, with our husbands. The questions were all about how these men supported their wives and how proud they are of our success. They chose me to participate. True to form, he didn't want to be part of it and made no effort at all. He came off really badly – I felt so humiliated.

He told me a week before the recorded interview, that he didn't know what to say and every question (which we had been given beforehand) he answered with little effort. He told me an hour before we went on, that I should not interrupt him, sit still and not talk over him. I should keep my answers short and not fluff around on camera, as I usually do, because no one would be interested in what I have to say anyways. I just wanted to cry. He really showed me his true colours that day and my heart was hurting. Regardless, we kept a smile throughout the interview. All the other husbands being interviewed were so enthusiastic and kept hugging their wives and smiling, saying beautiful things about their spouses, and you could see on their faces how proud they were. Mine was just bland and cold. It was awful. I tried to hide it all by laughing it off. He kept kicking my leg under the table whenever I spoke, because he wanted me to keep it short. That moment I felt more controlled than ever. My private life was controlled from the minute he found out that I was talking to another man. The only thing he could never get control of was my business. That was my thing, my baby, my job, my profession, my calling. Sitting there in that interview, I could feel the pain pumping through my veins. A situation I will never forget. The moment where my heart truly realised that this man was no longer good for me.

It was a never-ending story and I started wondering where I'd be if I had given Mike a chance. Maybe my husband wasn't right for me after all. I was exhausted and empty and I wanted to escape. I'd tried my best every day. I still put all my needs and desires to the side to make things right and have a happy marriage again. As a mother your kids are your first priority and the last thing I wanted for them was a broken family. They had the most incredible life here. Growing up near the beach, sunshine pretty much everyday, an incredible school system with an outstanding, empowering curriculum and wonderful opportunities growing up bilingual in a country that is safe. I wanted to fix our marriage for our boys; I did not want them to go through pain. I would rather keep my pain inside and have them grow up in a stable family. This seemed all realistic and doable in theory, but my heart was bleeding.

One morning he went off to the gym, but within ten minutes he was back. He stormed into the house and interrupted me while I was on a call. He was really angry and accused me of sleeping with Mike. He insisted that I had slept with him. I've never seen him so angry before. Something was up, something must have happened on the way to the gym. He said that if I just admitted it, then everything would be okay between us. He said he had proof and he knew that I had slept with him. He didn't want to tell me what it was, he wanted to hear it out of my mouth. I was so confused; I wondered if he'd hired a private detective, or had bugged my car. How on earth could he think that? There was absolutely no proof that it happened at all, because it never did.

This new intensity went on for two days and I was exhausted. I remembered that message I sent Stephanie, where I said I had slept with him to get her off my case. But surely he wouldn't have seen that. I mean, how? After Stephanie told me to delete every single conversation with her off my phone, I had nothing left from her. I went through every single scenario that night and I couldn't think of anything that would make him believe this accusation with such certainty. I knew he was trying to get something out of me, but it just didn't make any sense. I messaged Stephanie one evening to ask her if she had spoken to him. I thought maybe he had asked her and because she was now all about family values, she might have told him what I had said. She was the only person that knew all the details. And she was the only person who actually thought that I did have sex with him. She didn't reply to my message, even though I could see she had read it. That meant trouble. Still, I could not imagine – and I would put my hand in fire for this – even if my husband were to ask her, she would not betray me in such a horrific way and tell him what I'd said to her. I mean, what reason could she have to do so?

I woke up at around 3am on Valentine's Day, feeling scared and panicky. I could hardly breathe, I got hot and cold flashes and felt nauseous. My heart was racing super fast and the stress of this whole thing was really getting to me. I felt so sick. I woke him up and said: "Can we go downstairs and talk?" He just mumbled "Now? It's three in the morning." I wanted to open up and be completely honest and I wanted him to also be open with me. We went downstairs to the living room, being super quiet as the boys were sleeping. We sat in the dark on the sofa and I told him that I had seen Mike again last year, and that yes, I had feelings for him, but that I hadn't seen him since and I hadn't slept with him. I told him that he tried to sleep with me and that we had kissed and that I felt good around him. I also opened up about how it was always me reaching out to him and that he wasn't at all interested in me, other than physically. I apologised for getting back in contact with him and I had no excuse for it. Then I asked him why he was so sure that I had slept with him and asked if he had reached out to Stephanie.

He started crying and shaking and took my hand. He said: 'Yes Mel, I have been in contact with her."

Thinking about that moment, I can't recall any feelings just that I replied instantaneously: "You asked her if I had slept with him?" In my mind, I thought that this could never be right, why would she even pick up the phone when my husband was calling her?

He looked at me with eyes I've never seen in him before and again he said, "Yes, Mel, I have been in contact with Stephanie... since 2015."

The bomb dropped.

I couldn't quite comprehend what he had just told me. He fell to his knees on the floor and said with a whispering, choking kind of voice: "We have been sexually texting each other for the last 6 years".

The things that went through my head in that second were close to being numb, not feeling my body anymore and severe agony all rushing through my bloodstream. I felt like I had been pushed out of an aeroplane with no warning and no parachute. Sixty seconds of free fall, landing in a complete disaster. Survival felt impossible.

I just stood there, looked at him and I pushed the water bottle from the coffee table onto the floor. I cried. I couldn't feel my heart beating anymore. My voice disappeared. I felt like I was being ripped into one thousand pieces. I fell on the floor and screamed, into my hand, so I wouldn't wake up the boys. He came up to me and started saying something, I couldn't hear anything anymore.

Let me process that: My husband just told me that he had been having an affair with my best friend, Stephanie, for six years!

Happy Valentine's Day to me.

My world came crashing down. Six years! I had no words left to describe the heartache I was feeling that night. Stephanie. The person that I spoke to every single day. The woman I trusted more than anyone in the whole world. My rock, my bestest friend, the person that knew my deepest thoughts, feelings, fears and secrets. I would have walked through fire for her.

And my husband. The man who had gone practically insane when he thought I was having an affair. An affair that hadn't even really existed. The man that controlled me for over nine months, letting me think that I am a cheater. The man who promised me ten years ago that he would never break my heart. The father of my children. The man I followed wherever he wanted to go around the globe and back again. The man that I supported through all his decisions… The love of my life.

My man with my best girlfriend.

He sent Stephanie a message with my phone, telling her that I knew everything and that we didn't want to have any contact with her anymore. The amount of times he assured me that he had no feelings for her, and that it was all a game to him, were endless. So many situations were running through my head. When we were all in Germany together, or him in Germany on his own. How many times did they meet up? What on earth were they thinking?

Stephanie sent me a very long text message apologising for it all and trying to explain that she had big feelings for him and couldn't stop reaching out to him. I didn't respond. I was too broken.

My husband left for a business trip that morning. It was already 6am and the boys came down. How could I survive this? How could I move on with my day?

I remember dropping the boys at school and it felt like I had a huge sign on my forehead: *My husband cheated on me with my best friend and I trusted them like a naïve idiot.*

I called my closest friends as soon as I got home and told them – I am still so grateful to have incredible women in my life, that I can call day and night. Who are always there for me and would even jump on a plane to see me and support me.

Of course, all I saw were Valentine's Day messages everywhere that day. Love was in the air, but I was in a daze. The whole day was a complete blur of tears and disbelief. For months I had been treated like a villain – was berated constantly, spied on, lied to, controlled on a daily basis, manipulated even. My emotions were all over the place – utter disbelief and deep pain at the betrayal of the two people I had trusted the most in the world; and anger at the way he had treated me, knowing that he had actually been cheating on me for years, trying to blame it all on me, because of his secret guilt that I didn't know of.

When he came back, he basically told me that Stephanie had initiated the whole thing and that they had connected over a shared love for food when we moved back to Sydney in 2015. What? How could I not have seen this? He insisted that it had merely been a flirtation and that nothing had ever really happened.

That was the affair she had been having. We'd spoken about it and the man she had told me was just a random guy was actually my own husband! I felt so humiliated. So completely duped.

My husband and I had many conversations. He said he'd always told me that he didn't like her and that she was not my real friend. He told me over and over again that they hadn't ever been together physically. He said it was all over text and online. He completely threw her under the bus and told me she was revolting and that he didn't even like her. He mentioned that he wanted to cut her off all those years, but couldn't break it off with her in case she told me about it. It was like he was being held hostage by her. I didn't believe a word of that.

In some last ditch-effort to make some sense of it all, we went for marriage counselling. It was a bit of a sham really. He went into a kind of a spiral – at the gym all the time, teeth whitening, and he bought a fancy car. I realised that he had a really fragile ego and that because Stephanie wasn't around anymore to stroke it, he needed to get the attention somewhere else. He didn't have any true friends either, so there was no one for him to turn to. I almost felt sorry for him, but not quite.

In our therapy sessions, he went on and on about my 'affair'. I know now that I really hurt his ego. He just couldn't handle the fact that I had even looked at another man. It was too much for him. I get that – I know what I did was not innocent; even if Mike and I didn't have a physical relationship, my heart was involved. And I've always maintained that texting another person flirtatiously when you are in a relationship with someone, is cheating.

I discovered that Stephanie had been sharing information about Mike with him all along. I had lied to her about sleeping with Mike, a regrettable lie that made its way back to my husband. I can only guess that every message or screenshot I had sent to Stephanie about Mike, was sent to my husband. A part of me feels like Stephanie relished in portraying me as the person she wanted me to be, someone dishonourable. The situation had spiralled into sheer madness.

I needed to get out of the situation and tried to find a rental property nearby. He offered to leave the family house, but I did not want him to. I just needed to get out and clear my head, in a different environment. After two weeks of trying to find a rental I gave up and I convinced him to buy an investment property instead, in both of our names, as it would be an easier task as a married couple.

At this point I did not want to get a divorce because of our children and I wanted to give us a chance to fix this mess, of course. I wanted to move out immediately for a few months, so we weren't hanging around each other all the time, since we both worked from home. It took us two months to find something that was in our budget as an investment and also suitable for me and the boys to live in. A beautiful three bedroom apartment with a big balcony, right near the lakes, just a few minutes from our family home. Of course we spoke to the boys about our situation and explained that we both lied to each other and would need a little break to find each other again. The boys were adapting to this pretty well, they actually got quite excited about the new apartment and spending some time there with me.

It was a tough two months still living in the house, because nothing changed for either of us. I still felt controlled and guilty and on top of it I felt hurt, disrespected and worthless. All those years I built up my confidence on my own, trying to love and accept myself, so I could pass this love to the people around me and make them see their worth. And here I was, double betrayed, lied to and made to feel guilty for something that I haven't even done.

At that point I thought it couldn't get any worse. Little did I know…

INTROSPECTION

Betrayal and deception can stir up some intense emotions. It can also make you question numerous scenarios, experiences and feelings from the past and whether or not they were projected upon you or if they were self-inflicted, calling into question your self-worth.

1. Reflect on a time in your life when you felt a deep sense of betrayal or deception. How did this experience impact your trust in others and your overall emotional well-being? Consider the feelings of hurt, humiliation, and disbelief that often accompany such situations. How did you cope with these emotions and begin to rebuild your sense of trust?

2. Recall a time when you were falsely accused or made to feel guilty for something you didn't do. How did these accusations affect your self-esteem and self-worth? Reflect on the emotional toll of being unjustly blamed and how it

might have affected your confidence in your own judgement. How did you eventually find a way to validate your own feelings and assert your innocence?

3. Think about a situation where you discovered someone close to you had betrayed your trust. How did this impact your relationship with that person? Reflect on the struggle between healing and forgiveness. How did you decide whether to repair the relationship or distance yourself to protect your own well-being? What role did setting boundaries and communicating your feelings play in this process?

4. Consider a time when your sense of self-worth was deeply shaken by a betrayal or deception. Reflect on the steps you took to rebuild your self-esteem and redefine your identity. How did you work to separate your value from the actions of others? What strategies did you employ to remind yourself of your inherent worthiness and reclaim your sense of empowerment?

CHAPTER THIRTEEN | PICKING UP THE PIECES

"Just as the caterpillar thought the world was over, it became a butterfly. Embrace change, and make your comeback."
– Unknown

Just before my birthday in May, I moved into the apartment. I actually felt excited. I couldn't wait to just breathe, trying to sleep through the night and most of all not feeling like I was being spied on, recorded or constantly supervised, criticised and questioned. All that negativity was falling off and it was starting to feel really good.

I took a few things from our family home and I had to buy some furniture. My husband helped with the move and set up all the furniture, setting up the TV and all the other appliances. He made sure me and the boys had everything we needed and told me that he was just one call away. I was relieved he was acting that way, especially for the sake of the kids. Maybe he even realised at that point, that this could be the end of it all.

In order to fix our marriage I needed this break, some sanity, a breather. I assumed we both needed it. Our counsellor supported the move and the break as well and I was extremely happy that she actually suggested it in one of our sessions. My husband did not like the idea of me moving out, all he was worried about was that I would then go and see Mike again. And have an affair, with all the details that he completely made up in his mind.

Being fully settled in the apartment was so refreshing. I hung the towels the way I wanted to, I bought loads of pink scatter cushions, I had my girlfriends over, I played my music loud. I put inspirational pictures up, worked harder than I ever did, I was dancing like no one was watching and I enjoyed being my own me again. It was amazing. The intense guilt and scrutiny I had been living under after my flirtation was lifted. At least for a moment.

My boys loved it as well, they were so proud having two homes and telling all their friends how cool that was. I was so relieved. We shared the boys 50/50 and I experienced a whole new level of motherhood. Because I was feeling so free and light I could completely concentrate and connect deeper with my boys in the weeks that I had them. I planned all the fun things for them, invited their friends over and pretty much enjoyed my time with my babies on my own. The weekends were tough, as we normally did something as a family and wherever I rocked up with the boys, I was surrounded by families, but I guess I would just get used to it.

The week I didn't have the boys, I planned all my appointments, meetings, styling sessions, catching up with friends and did the cleaning and the shopping, so when the boys came back, everything was done and I could pour all my energy into them.

I loved my new temporary 'home' and I was hoping to find some answers, some time to digest, recover and heal. I discovered the area and started running around the beautiful lake nearby. Everything felt so new, so heavy, but still light. I really wanted to work on our marriage and fix our family. After everything that happened, I wanted to forgive and make it work. I knew that with time, this could all be possible. One morning, I was running my new track and I saw a huge swarm of little butterflies. All of a sudden, they were everywhere. I stopped, took my earpods out and sat by the water, watching them fly. At that moment, I realised that life is so beautiful with all its ups and downs. I believed strongly that I would find my path, wherever it might lead me. I promised myself that I would not give up on my dreams, I would not give up on giving my best and fighting for everything that is important to me. I promised myself that I would get through this with strength and grace.

Like a butterfly ...
You cannot embrace a "new you" until you release the old.

Forever reminded that butterflies are embracing inner beauty and strengths.... You spread your wings and you grow into something amazing.

Butterflies have become a very meaningful symbol for me since then. They represent growth and new beginnings – exactly what I've become accustomed to, especially in moving back and forth between Germany and Australia and starting my life over each time. Butterflies are also synonymous with transformation and this season of our lives sure was all about transformation. The way a caterpillar closes itself off from the world, and morphs into something new and beautiful, resonates with me on such a deep level. They encourage us to listen to our innate wisdom, to trust and guide ourselves through tough times to emerge on the other side stronger, better and more beautiful than before.

Guided by our counsellor, we had to plan a date once a week, and one family day. We met up for lunch every wednesday just him and me, but it didn't really turn into a nice experience at all. He made me feel guilty for leaving the family home and he could not handle that I, for once, was feeling better. It felt like every time I had crashed on the floor with no strength left, he would eventually pick me up. If I was strong and confident, coping with it and being happy and excited, he did everything to see me back on the floor like a mouse that was caught in a trap, so he could be the one picking me up again.

His ego was crushed, and he just couldn't let go of what I had done. He called me all the time, drove past the apartment often to see if Mike's car was there or the lights were still on late at night. If he saw I was online after 10pm, he'd call or text and ask me what I was doing and who I was texting. I couldn't believe that he was still carrying on in that way, given that he was the one who had an affair for so long.

But, so many things started to make sense – Stephanie's strange behaviour on our incentive trip in 2020 was because they had actually slept together a week or so before. I still don't know the depth of their physical relationship and I know that it couldn't have been that prolific since they were in different countries, but we went to Germany often enough, and he also went there on business, so they had plenty of opportunities. Stephanie's husband all but confirmed some of the details, even though I didn't want to hear it all. He even sent me some of the images from the Instagram account that my husband and Stephanie set up just to share pictures between them. I didn't look at them. There was a lot of evidence that their relationship had been far from innocent.

When Stephanie had told me that therapy was a bad idea, it was really because she didn't want my husband to confess. When she told me to send screenshots of my conversations with Mike so she could keep them safe when I had to delete them, it was so she could show them to my husband. She broke off contact with me because I was telling her that he and I were working hard at our marriage and that I was falling back in love with him. She obviously couldn't bear that.

It took a year for him to finally admit that he had actually slept with her, but even in his confession he blamed her. He said he hadn't wanted to and that the whole experience was gross. I mean come on! You don't ever sleep with someone by accident. There is always intent. I am still befuddled by their relationship. He never liked her – always commenting on how loud and crass she was. As far as I knew, he couldn't stand her. Funny how far men go, to get their ego stroked.

I oscillated between thoroughly enjoying my freedom, and absolute devastation at their betrayal. There's a girl code, isn't there? Surely your best friend's husband is off limits? Surely?

After about three months of living on my own, I couldn't take the guilt-tripping any more and decided to move back into the family home. That way I'd be showing him that I still love him, he's happy and he could stop questioning me about what I was doing whenever I was alone without the kids. He would constantly say things like: "If you loved me, you would be here," or "If you loved us as a family, you would come back and live here." So I thought I would give our marriage one final chance and move back home.

I packed up all my stuff and organised to get it all moved back to the house. It was quite a big job since the investment property was on the third floor. I even contacted the real estate agents to arrange for tenants to move in once I was out.

Back at the house, the first day I'm back, I arrived to see him standing in the garage. All I could think was "Am I parking the car correctly? Is he going to have a tantrum if he's not happy with the way I park?" I never bumped the car and in any case, it was my car. But when I got out of the car he just hugged me and we both cried.

He took me upstairs where he'd run me a bath with candles everywhere. He poured me a glass of wine and said "You go have a bath, I'll take care of the kids and then we can talk later." So, I took a bath and cried some more. I reassured myself that this was the right decision. But then… we picked up right where we left off.

The questions about Mike started again: "Did he message you? Did you see him again? Are you still in contact? Can you show me he's blocked?" I couldn't believe it. I never once asked him if he blocked Stephanie or continued to talk to her. Never.

It was too late for me to go back to the investment property. All my stuff had been moved and the new tenants had already signed the contract to move in. I simply had to give my all, wholeheartedly, to salvage our marriage and keep our family together. It was a tricky situation because I wanted to be with him and prove my love for him but at the same time I didn't want to be with him, especially when he became controlling, accusatory, and suspicious of me. At times, however, he was the complete opposite and would ignore me for no reason at all. It was like nothing had changed and I couldn't believe how quickly his old behaviours returned.

Nevertheless, I had promised myself I would give our relationship a fighting chance for twelve months and give it 150%. I would be the best wife and mother I could be and if we were still in the same position by February, I would leave the marriage. Then I could at least say I gave it my all. Just twelve months… we can do it.

For Father's Day, I decided to surprise him and the boys with a weekend away as a family. I used money that I had set aside from my beauty business to book the holiday so that he wouldn't see it on our shared accounts. I found a beautiful resort on the Gold Coast that we had never been to before and booked a long weekend for us. I rang up his boss and arranged for him to have two days off for the trip. I organised everything – I packed a suitcase for him and the boys, packed the car with snacks for the drive and wrote him a long note in his card telling him that even though we've been going through these struggles, we can have this holiday and enjoy it together. I explained that everything was organised and we would go and celebrate fathers day together.

I only told the kids at the very last minute so that they wouldn't spoil the surprise. The boys were so excited, they gave him the card and suitcase. He started reading it and immediately looked up at me to say "I can't go on holiday, I have to work." So I quickly explained that I'd spoken to his boss and he had time off – everything was organised. He continued to complain, "I can't just leave." He also questioned me about where I got the money from to book the trip, saying that I must have booked it for Mike and he didn't want to come. "I knew you had secret money... You have a secret stash somewhere." He went on and on... "The only reason you moved back home is because he dumped you. He doesn't want you." I just couldn't make it right for this man.

We did eventually end up going and he sat by the pool with his laptop, working. It was fine, I actually expected it. It just meant that I could spend more quality time with the kids. He was taking offence to whatever I was wearing. He didn't like it when guys looked at me, which I didn't even notice.

One evening, we were sitting at the restaurant in an uncomfortable silence. There was a couple about our age sitting next to us with their kids and they were having a great time, chatting and eating. The kids were all playing and I decided to go over and introduce myself to the mum, unable to take the silence at my own dinner table. I invited them to join us at our table and we had a really nice night. The kids all got along really well and we even took them out into the city later before heading back to the hotel.

When we got back to our room, my husband had a massive tantrum. He accused me of being interested in the other guy because I invited them over and had a conversation with him. All of this was completely out of the blue. He was so close to leaving me there and taking the kids home. I managed to convince him to get himself together and not do that to the boys. It was an absolute nightmare of a trip. An epic fail. I felt so disappointed and sad. I was giving it my all and actually did not expect anything from him, just that he would finally let go of what was and try as well, to make this work for all of us.

I kept reminding myself that I agreed to this. I promised myself twelve months. I had to give it my best shot. I didn't let this trip backfire and I just started to swallow it all down again; try to make everything right again. I started to think again, that it's my fault, that he reacted like that. That I couldn't give him what he wanted and needed. I put on a pair of sweatpants and one of his nightshirts and sneakers, and decided I'd just run around like that. I was slowly fading away on the inside. I kept thinking about moving back to the investment property, even though I knew I couldn't. I was still holding on to this tiny string of hope, that we could make it work and be happy again.

I poured myself into looking after my kids and my team. By the time November came, we needed full focus again to reach our goals. After last year's near miss, I knew I needed to pull out all the stops to reach our targets and earn our bonuses. And we did! I was so happy and so proud of my team. He was there with me and cheered me on, I think he really understood that this meant a lot to me and those women.

That Christmas I decided I wanted to pull out all the stops for the boys and make it a really special Christmas for them. We all had a tough year. In fact, it was so special and they loved it so much that they still talk about it today. However, for me and my husband, it was a nightmare.

I really made it a beautiful Christmas. I was so broken inside that I wanted to do something that would bring me joy and that was seeing my boys happy; making unforgettable memories for them. We were never really big on buying lots of presents so I splurged a little and bought a few more presents than we normally would, and I got them all the things they were wishing for. Nothing too expensive, we like to keep it low-key with their toys. I wrapped them up beautifully and wrote Santa's letter for them. I decorated the tree and the house, I put lights up everywhere – I was determined to make this the best Christmas ever! My husband, on the other hand, was not.

He wasn't at all involved in any preparation for the holidays and spent the Christmas season complaining. He complained about how much money I spent on presents and decorations, he complained about how he thought I was "overdoing it" and all this stuff was "not necessary". I put the boys in matching t-shirts and made everything look perfect. I took heaps of pictures so I could remember this Christmas – willing myself to not feel so torn and broken inside.

He complained when I took photos of the boys opening their presents, mumbling about how it was just going straight up on social media to show off this fake event and the fake family that doesn't exist. I look at the photos from that year and my boys have the most excited faces. That's all that counts for me.

I prepared a buffet-style meal for us because that's what the boys wanted. I set the table exquisitely and boys loved that too. I had bought little boxes that I decorated with each of their names – one each for the kids and one for my husband. Inside, I had put a hand-written letter for each of them saying something individual, my gratitude and a little end-of-year message. He showed no emotion and didn't even say thank you. Nothing…

I swallowed back my tears, feeling so completely and utterly numb. I felt so alone, worthless and hurt, this wasn't home for me anymore. This wasn't the man I used to adore. Why on earth was I doing all this? Going to all of this trouble to make Christmas a special occasion? I let it go. I continued trying to be the best version of myself. No regrets.

We spent New Year's Eve in a hotel in the city with the boys, taking them out to see the fireworks. I got very emotional, hiding my pain and started to reflect on my year. It was hard to find gratitude in the simple things, because the simple things turned into doubt, stress and hurtful conversations. Wherever we were, whatever we tried, it was pretty much the same thing. Complaining and more questions about Mike. I still don't know what this all looked like in my husband's head. Based on all the questions he would ask about if we went to this place or that restaurant, it was clearly more elaborate than what we actually had together.

Valentine's Day finally rolled around. It had been twelve months of trying and working on our marriage. I was making a big effort to pick up the pieces and get to a happy place again. Even though he continued to question me about Mike, I could see he was also making an effort in his own way. Yet, it still wasn't what I needed from him or what he needed from me because he simply couldn't forgive me. He just couldn't. No matter what, this would always be between us; we can never take this back. And he couldn't let it go either. I think it hit his ego big time knowing that Mike was a very high-profile professional, as well as the money and authority that came with his specific title.

Valentine's Day has become a bit like my birthday now – it's an emotional trigger and I just don't enjoy the day. I didn't want it to become a trigger, so that year I approached it with an open mind. My husband told me he had booked something for us to celebrate and arranged a babysitter for the kids. I was excited to see what he'd come up with. I'd been making the effort to prove I still wanted our marriage: cooking for him, making breakfast in bed, doing all the things he wanted, planning the Father's Day holiday and organising a beautiful Christmas. Now, one year after admitting to his affair, it was his chance to show the effort he was making and prove to me he felt just as committed to the marriage as I was.

He didn't let me in on what the plans were, all he had said was that I needed to get ready in the afternoon and we would leave the house around four-thirty and dinner would be around six. At midday I made a light salad for lunch because I didn't want to be starving by the time dinner came but I also didn't want to overeat – I'm still very conscious about what I put in my body. I was sitting in my office, doing some work while I ate when he came in and passed some hurtful comments about my body, something he often did thinking it was funny. With everything I'd been through with my body, I didn't think it was funny and he knew that. We had had so many conversions about how his comments were hurtful to me and they would drag me down. Especially with everything we'd been through that year, I was shocked that he thought what he said was appropriate at that moment.

I burst into tears and shut my office door, repeatedly reminding myself to breathe. He came back in and started going on about how I was overreacting. He had no idea of the expectations I had for that day and for him. I felt like I needed to just stay quiet and not be an extra burden and let this happen all over again. I left the situation and went to go get ready.

I had bought a brand new dress for the occasion, did my makeup and I looked great. Everything was perfect. I went downstairs to ask him to zip up my dress. He was waiting for me, all dolled up too. He was wearing a nice suit and he smelled amazing. I showered him with compliments, and got excited about our date night. All he said to me after zipping up my dress was "Are you ready now?" No compliment on my dress or how I looked. Nothing.

His mood continued in the car – he didn't say anything, didn't hold my hand. When I tried to hold his hand, he just pushed it away. While we were passing through the city, his comments started: "Mike this" and "Mike that." All I could think was "this is not going to go well." It went on the whole night. "This restaurant is not fancy enough for you. Mike probably took you to fine-dining places and rooftop bars. It's probably not enough for you. You feel embarrassed to be here with me now." ...Where was this all coming from? I was tired of explaining myself to him, for something I didn't do. It was non-stop, but I didn't say anything. I just left it. I didn't have the strength anymore. After dinner at about 9pm, we called it a night and I told him I wanted to go home.

I cried in the car on the way home and I told him that I was actually really disappointed. He had this chance to make up for last Valentine's Day, why couldn't he be more sensible about it. I told him off for not giving me any reassurance that he still wanted to be with me or that I looked pretty, he knew that's what I wanted to hear. It's what makes me feel loved. His response was: "Yeah, exactly. And that's why I didn't say anything because it's what you want to hear. So I'm not saying anything." It was intentional, spiteful even. That's not love.

That night I made the decision to separate. I couldn't deal with it anymore. I tried my best, and gave my full effort to make it work. I did my twelve months. I tried, that's what counted for me. I really tried. But here we were, once again on Valentine's Day, in the exact same place as we were a year ago. It was time to call it off. I was broken inside, still trying to grieve from the double betrayal, but also making an effort for something that would never work again. We were broken. I know he was, too. I was scared and devastated at the same time. And the hardest part actually followed from that day on. But I was ready for it.

INTROSPECTION

There is an intense pain that is felt deep inside when someone betrays you. Forgiveness is so important, but it's not easy at all. There's a saying that forgiving someone is for you, telling the person you've forgiven them is for them.

1. How do you cope with the intense pain and emotional turmoil that comes from being betrayed by someone you trusted? Take a moment to reflect on the impact of betrayal on your well-being and relationships. How can you embrace the healing power of forgiveness, not as an excuse for the betrayer's actions, but as a way to liberate yourself from the burden of carrying resentment and anger?

2. When forgiveness feels like an insurmountable task, how can you begin the process of letting go and finding inner peace? Reflect on the steps you can take to nurture self-compassion and create a safe space for healing. How can seeking support from loved ones or professional counsellors be instrumental in guiding you towards forgiveness and emotional restoration?

3. What does forgiveness mean to you, and how do you distinguish it from reconciliation? Take a moment to explore the complexities of forgiveness as a personal journey of growth and healing. How can you set healthy boundaries while extending forgiveness to others, ensuring your emotional well-being remains a priority in the process?

4. How can you find the strength to forgive someone who has betrayed you without expecting an apology or acknowledgment of their actions? Reflect on the power of forgiveness as an act of self-empowerment rather than relying on external validation. How can you release the emotional attachment to the betrayal and embrace forgiveness as a means to reclaim your own peace and happiness?

CHAPTER FOURTEEN | LETTING GO

"Falling down is not a failure. Failure comes when you stay where you have fallen."

– Socrates

Well, it's been a few years since all that happened and I am still recovering. Of course, I need to take responsibility for my part in the breakdown of my marriage. Betrayal is betrayal after all. I'm not going to try to downplay mine. No one is to blame here at all.

My husband left me and the boys in Australia, just a few months after separating. He is now back in Germany, living with another woman and her children. Whether he is happy or not, I don't know. What I do know is that he will never forgive me. As far as he is concerned, I am to blame for everything. I'm devastated for my boys, because he is an amazing dad, and of course they miss and love him dearly. His guilt has continued over the years. I can't speak for him and I won't judge him either for the decision he made to leave them, but in my eyes he ran away from his own insecurities and responsibilities, and not to mention the grief. You need time to heal after a breakup and he sadly never did. I truly hope he will understand this one day and face his issues, instead of hiding from them. I truly wish only the best for him, he is the father of my children after all.

As for Stephanie, well, I haven't ever heard her side of the story. All I have is my husband's account, which places the blame firmly on her. I also have some stories from mutual friends. So, I pieced together a few details from that. I was never interested in talking it through with her. I don't blame her for it though, I never did and I never will. I know her well enough to realise that she had big feelings for him, stronger than she felt for our friendship obviously. And he fed off those feelings. It really crushed me, especially from her side, but I moved on and I feel incredibly detoxed from cutting her out of my life.

I know deep down that no one intentionally wanted to hurt anyone.

He needed his ego to be stroked and I just wasn't doing that. I found a passion and a purpose. I've built a strong international empire and a solid business that taught me to love myself the way I am. My self-worth gave me the power and strength that I needed to let this marriage go. I became a strong, independent woman and that meant I didn't need him as much as I did years ago. So, in essence, I betrayed him long before I met Mike.

Every day is better than the last, and I am gradually gaining my strength back. I believe that while Mike wasn't the right person for me by any means, his presence in my life taught me that there is something better than what I was getting from my husband. He showed me that I could be interesting, that I am attractive and worthy of attention. For that, I am grateful. Forever. If it wasn't for him, I would have probably never found out about the affair between my husband and my best friend. Without knowing it, he opened my eyes.

I realised while writing this book that there has been a pattern of upliftment in my life - from empowering women to learn the German language and culture to building little human potential through my years at various child care institutions, and of course, as a business leader. The process of speaking into a person's life to give them the tools to be fully themselves and to reach their individual potential is an honour and a joy.

Women are incredible creatures, filled with a strength that is deep and can be intimidating. I hope that every woman out there has the opportunity to realise her own strength. That every woman gets to realise her true worth. It doesn't matter what your circumstances are in life – you are amazing and you deserve to be loved in a way that brings out the very best in you.

There are so many hidden talents and incredible abilities inside of you, girl. Go and believe in yourself, you never know what's around the corner. And always remember, falling down is not 'failure', it's part of life, it's necessary for success and essential for growth. Without pain and struggles, we can't grow.

I am so grateful to all the women in my life that have uplifted me, that have validated me and championed me. The women who were there with me, every single step and guided me through all the unwritten chapters of this journey. I will always be grateful for my sponsor who saw something in me that I didn't know I had, and for the incredible support of every one of my team that worked so hard alongside me. For my closest and best friends who guided me through all of this during the last few years, you mean the world to me. Without the support of these women I wouldn't be here.

I'm thankful beyond words for my top leaders for stepping up and helping me through the toughest time of my life. For helping me guide the team, run events, take over Zoom calls and just be there for everyone in a time where I was crashing down from heartache, concentrating on my children and trying to save my marriage. THANK YOU **TEAM GERYOUNY**!

As for me, I'm ready to move on and live a life that is filled with joy, love, gratitude, happiness and style (of course). I've been able to reinvent myself many times and while it can be a bit scary, I know I can do it. I've always been brave and patient. Despite being betrayed by the two most loved people in my life, I feel like I haven't lost faith. I have always trusted easily and people called me naïve, but for me this is a beautiful thing. I'm grateful for who I have become through this time as a mother, friend and leader. I know that there will always be people who judge me or my life and my decisions. I learnt a long time ago that these people are not in my shoes, they are not paying my bills, they can't see through my heart. I take full responsibility for my own actions and I'm totally fine with it. I couldn't feel happier and more at ease since I started not caring about other people judging me. I will always and forever work hard for my children and myself, as I don't have anyone to fall back on, I am the back up and this is extremely empowering for me. The year of separation was hard, but it was also incredibly empowering. So many new opportunities opened up for me, from working as a style icon for a fashion company, expanding my travel destinations, meeting new people and getting signed by a model agency. The next chapter is yet to be written, but I know it's filled with adventure.

GOING OUT IN STYLE

"Since love grows within you, so beauty grows. For love is the beauty of the soul."

— Saint Augustine

I've always loved fashion — even as a little four-year-old girl, I simply had to have numerous outfits throughout the day. From dressing my Barbie dolls and experimenting with my own clothes while growing up, to expressing myself through fashion with multiple wardrobe changes each day as an adult — fashion and style have always been at the core of who I am.

I'm passionate about empowering women to look and feel their best. As a lifestyle and beauty influencer, personal stylist, model and business owner, I've made it my mission to help women find their style, get on the right path, and achieve their dreams.

Fashion is more than just a few items of clothing - it's a way to make you reflect who you are on the inside, outside. It's a way to create your own personal statement and can be a huge confidence booster.

This is one of the reasons I love styling people; seeing the difference that a few well-chosen items can make is astounding.

With a love for fashion, makeup, and all things beauty-related, I've built a successful career in the industry, working with thousands of women around the world to boost their confidence, rediscover their beauty, and find their own happiness within themselves.

As a mom, I understand how easy it can be to lose sight of yourself and feel overwhelmed. That's why I'm here to share my knowledge and expertise with you.

Being a personal stylist allows me to be free in my own world and styling people brings me so much joy. While I always had a keen eye for fashion, the styling course I did helped to solidify my knowledge as a stylist through theory and pick up some industry tips and tricks. Plus, understanding the language to use when styling someone was instrumental in the creation of my approach to styling my clients. Taking that course was one of the most rewarding experiences ever.

I wish I had taken the course sooner. All my life, I never felt like I was good enough. I put this off because I didn't think I could do it, I wasn't enough to do it. I guess I just needed time to discover my self-worth.

The same goes for my modelling career. If you told young Mel she would be modelling at the age of forty, she wouldn't believe you one bit. So many people told me I should get into modelling. I eventually did – when I was over forty and I'm so glad that I did. My only regret is that I didn't listen to my inner voice all those years ago and start my beauty career sooner and follow my passion.

I want to show women that you can do anything at any age. I want women to be empowered and inspired to take action and follow their dreams. You are never too old to model. You are never too old to change career paths. You are never too old to try something new. Do the things that light up your soul. If I can change my clothes two or three times a day because it makes me happy, you can do whatever it is that brings you joy.

My family used to always tease me for changing my outfits a couple of times a day, but what it really was, was me expressing my identity. Deep down, I knew who I was from a young age – even if it took me all these years to realise it. I don't dress the way I do to impress anyone. I do it to express myself.

It's difficult to explain because I now know that a lot of people really struggle with shopping for clothes and getting dressed in the morning. I see it all the time with my clients. For me, on the other hand, it's easy and I get so much enjoyment out of it. Style is so much more than fashion. So much more than just clothes.

With my styling service, I get to educate women on fashion and we talk about styling for their unique body, lifestyle and preferences. We do a wardrobe edit to remove pieces that just don't work for them and to identify any gaps that need to be filled with some wardrobe staples. We get to go shopping so I can show them what really compliments their body type and what doesn't. We look at colours to find the perfect palette that works for them, and which colours to avoid. I get to share some tips for mixing and matching because you really don't need a lot of clothes to make your wardrobe work for you.

Shopping for clothes can be extremely overwhelming for a lot of people and I want to take the stress and overwhelm out of that experience. I also want to help people save money when it comes to their wardrobe. So often when I'm doing a wardrobe edit, I find numerous pieces of clothing with the tags still attached! A lot of the time, people buy clothes from a place of emotion or because the retail staff convince them it looks good.

Your wardrobe really only needs a certain amount of basics that fit your body shape and lifestyle and maybe a few trend pieces if you wish. Just being given a few pointers in the right direction can be the difference between you having the perfect look, and being just off. That is where I come in, to help guide you in the right direction for your unique style and fashion.

There's something so uplifting and empowering about a successful shopping experience where you are treated like an absolute queen – that's all I want for my clients. I want them to walk into the store with me and feel confident, knowing exactly what they need and what works for their body. It's also incredibly empowering to know what doesn't work for you, and avoid those clothes with confidence.

All these things are incredibly important to me and to my clients too. In fact, I have never left a client saying that she wasn't happy or satisfied with the garment choices we discovered on the day. They all go home feeling like queens! And I get so excited to see them again for the next season or a special occasion.

I pride myself on being completely honest with my clients, telling them when something truly looks amazing and when something really isn't a good fit for them. I aim to create a safe space for them. It's something I'm very passionate about too. I will never let a client go home with an outfit that doesn't look absolutely amazing.

I get asked all the time if personal styling is only for rich people – absolutely not! Styling is for everyone. Normal people like you and me. My clients are women who want to treat themselves to a styling experience when they are going through a tough time, like a divorce, or new mums wanting to find their style after having a baby, women who want to boost their confidence through their wardrobe, or women who simply want to spoil themselves with a styling experience for no real reason at all.

I strive to make every shopping trip, every wardrobe edit and every conversation an uplifting and empowering experience. I can't wait to style you too so you can experience it all for yourself.

BE TRUE TO YOURSELF | My Tips for Finding Your True Style

In today's fast-paced world, fashion trends come and go at a lightning pace. It can be tempting to jump on the latest bandwagon and invest in all the latest trends, but at the end of the day, true style is about much more than just keeping up with the latest fads. It's about finding your own personal style that reflects your unique personality and makes you feel confident and beautiful. Here are some tips for finding your personal style and staying true to yourself, rather than just buying into fashion trends all the time.

Know yourself: The first step in developing your personal style is to know yourself. Think about your likes and dislikes, your personality, and your lifestyle. What do you want your clothing to say about you? What makes you feel confident and comfortable? By getting clear on these things, you'll be able to start honing in on your personal style.

Experiment: Once you have a sense of what you like and what suits you, start experimenting with different styles and looks. Don't be afraid to try new things, but also don't be afraid to say no to trends that don't feel authentic to you. The goal is to find a style that makes you feel confident and comfortable, not to simply follow the latest fashion trends.

Invest in quality pieces: Instead of buying into every trend that comes along, invest in quality pieces that you know you'll wear and love for years to come. Look for classic, timeless pieces that you can mix and match with other items in your wardrobe. This will help you create a versatile wardrobe that reflects your personal style, rather than just a collection of fleeting trends.

Get inspiration: Look for inspiration in unexpected places. Follow bloggers and influencers who have a style that resonates with you, but also look to art, music, and nature for inspiration. Don't be afraid to take risks and think outside the box when it comes to developing your personal style.

Embrace your uniqueness: Finally, remember that true style is about embracing your uniqueness and being true to yourself. Don't try to conform to someone else's idea of what is fashionable or stylish. Instead, embrace your own personal style and let it shine through in everything you wear.

Developing your personal style is about more than just following fashion trends. It's about knowing yourself, experimenting, investing in quality pieces, getting inspiration from unexpected places, and embracing your uniqueness. By doing these things, you'll be able to find a style that reflects your personality and makes you feel confident and beautiful, no matter what the latest fashion trends may be.

GRATITUDE

My dearest Lui Avalon and Levi Ayden,

The greatest and biggest love of all. You make my life complete. Being your mother makes me the happiest girl alive. Leading and guiding you through life is my biggest honour. A mother's love for her boys is special and I feel this every day. The love I receive from the two of you is endless and unconditional.

You healed my soul in so many ways. There will never be a second in my life that I won't be there for you and give it my all and my best to be the greatest role model and mother I can be. Giving birth to you tiny, little monkeys and seeing you grow up into smart, kind, loving boys makes my heart sing.

I love all the nights we talk for ages, being silly, laughing and crying together, dancing around the house and eating candy at midnight. I love seeing you developing your own personalities and exploring friendships. I love how we practise gratitude every night, to keep being focused on our blessings. I love how we treat each other the way we want to be treated and that we can talk about anything and everything.

I cherish each holiday with you two, showing you the world, teaching you new things and expanding your horizon. I'm thankful for every tear that I cried for and with you, happy tears, worry tears, sad tears.

My biggest achievement in life is being your mother. Teaching you to express your emotions and feelings. Helping you become strong, mindful and kind men with grateful hearts. Leading you with respect and love.

I know you both will be reading this one day, when the time is right. I want you to know that you were created from a place of love, that you are loved beyond words by so many around you and that my love for you is infinite.

I love you to the moon and back and to the universe and around eternity and I would go around the sun ten billion times, just to find you.

FOREVER and ALWAYS.

Mama

Our life is like a swing, it needs to stretch back to make us fly higher

– Musafir

Mel's Bio:

Mel Hoehne, a single mother of two delightful boys, is a highly successful entrepreneur whose business has taken her around the world as a speaker and business leader. With a background in teaching, Mel spent over 20 years in child care before embarking on a career in the beauty industry where she achieved incredible growth for her business, displaying a tenacity and knack for empowering women through her business as well as her team members. Mel is also a sought-after model and a personal stylist. Throughout her life, Mel has made it her mission to uplift groups of women, whether in her native Germany or in her adopted country of Australia. She's an intrepid go-getter with a growth mindset, a heart of gold and an intrinsic drive to succeed at whatever she does.

www.ingramcontent.com/pod-product-compliance
Lightning Source LLC
Chambersburg PA
CBHW070647120526
44590CB00013BA/857